Entertaining in Grand Style

SAVOIR FAIRE OF A PARISIAN CHEF

EXECUTIVE DIRECTOR
Suzanne Tise-Isoré
Style & Design Collection

EDITORIAL COORDINATION
Sarah Rozelle

EDITORIAL ASSISTANT
Lucie Lurton

GRAPHIC DESIGN
Bernard Lagacé
ASSISTED BY
Alain Bourdon

TRANSLATED FROM THE FRENCH BY
Barbara Mellor

RECIPES TRANSLATED FROM THE FRENCH BY
Carmella Abramowitz Moreau

COPYEDITING AND PROOFREADING
Helen Downey

PRODUCTION
Élodie Conjat-Cuvelier

COLOR SEPARATION
IGS, France

PRINTED BY
Tien Wah Press, Singapore

Simultaneously published in French as
Traditions gourmandes, à la table des grandes maisons françaises
© Flammarion S.A., Paris, 2013

English-language edition
© Flammarion S.A., Paris, 2013

Dépôt légal: 10/2013
13 14 15 3 2 1
ISBN: 978-2-08-020136-2

PAGE 4
Menu of a dinner given at the British Embassy in Paris in 2007
to mark the fiftieth anniversary of the first State Visit of Her Majesty the Queen.

PAGE 6
Chef James Viaene at the British Ambassador's Residence in Paris
where he worked for over forty years.

Entertaining in Grand Style

SAVOIR FAIRE OF A PARISIAN CHEF

Chef James Viaene

TEXT Nadège Forestier
PHOTOGRAPHY BY Francis Hammond

Flammarion

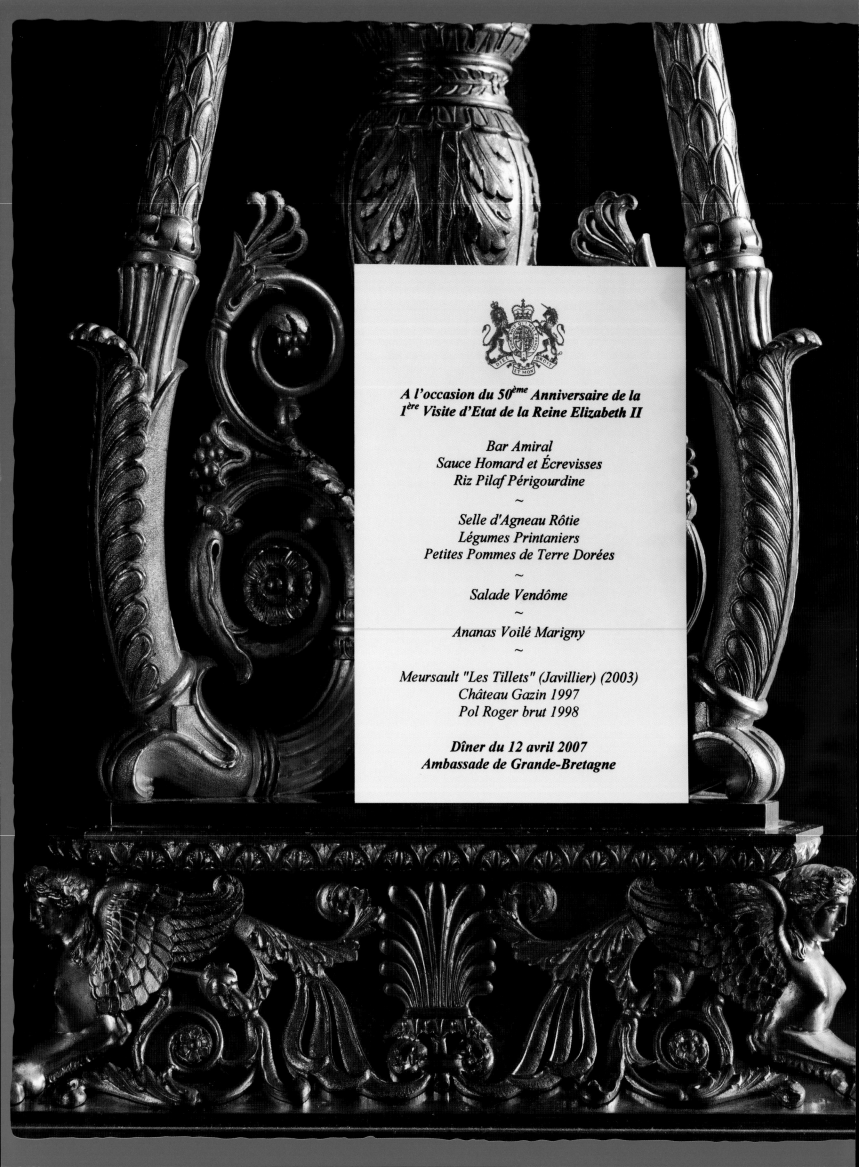

A l'occasion du 50ème Anniversaire de la
1ère Visite d'Etat de la Reine Elizabeth II

Bar Amiral
Sauce Homard et Écrevisses
Riz Pilaf Périgourdine

~

Selle d'Agneau Rôtie
Légumes Printaniers
Petites Pommes de Terre Dorées

~

Salade Vendôme

~

Ananas Voilé Marigny

~

Meursault "Les Tillets" (Javillier) (2003)
Château Gazin 1997
Pol Roger brut 1998

Dîner du 12 avril 2007
Ambassade de Grande-Bretagne

$\mathcal{C}$ontents

16   A CHEF'S VOCATION

Aged seventeen, James Viaene applies to be an apprentice in the kitchens of the French Embassy in London. He was warned that it could be a tough life, but chefs for great private houses were highly sought after.

26   PARIS SOCIETY AT HOME

James cooked for the most select and distinguished tables in Paris for fifty-eight years and his knowledge of the fads and foibles, habits and preferences of high society is second to none. In private households, a chef must also be able to rise to the challenge of the most unexpected demands and understand the codes that govern individual tastes.

68   TOWARD A NEW LUXURY

On May 30, 1968, General de Gaulle drove up the Champs-Elysées to the cheers of thousands of Parisians. On the surface, society life continued as before, and some forty chefs still manned the kitchens of the grand residences on the avenue Foch. But their days were numbered, and slowly but surely changes in society were eventually to lead to their complete transformation.

96   THE GREAT TRADITION TODAY

In 1970, James Viaene went to work at the British Embassy and could scarcely have imagined that he would still be there forty years later. It was here that he was able to give full rein to all he had learned in the grand households in which he had worked, and to allow his skills to truly blossom.

I CAN THINK OF NO ONE BETTER QUALIFIED THAN JAMES VIAENE TO SHARE WITH US THE RECIPES of the great houses of Paris, and to put Parisian fine dining and entertaining in their proper context. I was the last of ten British ambassadors to France who were fortunate enough to have James as their chef. He came, of course, with a remarkable pedigree, having begun his career at the age of thirteen as a pastry chef in Senlis, served The Duke and Duchess of Windsor and worked for Michel and Hélène David-Weill. When my wife and I arrived in Paris at the beginning of 2007, James was already seventy, well beyond the normal retirement age. We persuaded him to stay on for one more ambassador. After almost five years together, we left on the same day. It was a privilege, a joy, and an immense reassurance to have James in charge of the kitchen throughout that time.

Shortly before we left, the President of the Republic generously recognized James's remarkable service, both to cuisine and to Franco-British relations, by conferring on him the Légion d'honneur. Prime Minister François Fillon kindly made the presentation at the Embassy, and attended a celebratory dinner—with James as fellow guest of honor—to mark the event. It was a sign of the impact James had made, and the affection in which he is held, that all my living predecessors came for the event, as did Lady Soames, Winston Churchill's daughter, representing her late husband and James's first ambassador, Sir Christopher Soames.

This remarkable book tells many stories. Of course, there are James's wonderful recipes, beautifully illustrated. There is also a social history of Paris over the last half century, illustrated by James's vignettes and some of the remarkable dinners which he prepared. The book shows, too, how formal dining has declined in recent years, even if the quality of the tables and of the wines which Parisian hostesses serve for their guests remains, in my view, as high as ever. With a few exceptions, large, formal lunches and dinners have become the reserve of the French state— epitomized by the Elysée Palace and the Hôtel de Matignon—and of the bigger embassies. At the British Embassy, the dining table for fifty-eight people and the magnificent *surtout de table* are rarely used these days, even if we often seated a hundred or more at smaller round tables, and the number of events—breakfasts, lunches, dinners, receptions, tea parties—is as large as ever. So it should be: the importance of hospitality and a warm welcome to diplomacy, understanding, and relationships remains undiminished.

James Viaene's triumphs are so well explained in this beautiful book that there is no need for me to repeat the story. Part of the irony, and charm, of James's tenure at the British Ambassador's Residence is that, despite staying over forty years, and despite having a quintessentially English name, he has yet to be heard speaking a word of English. Exceptions that prove the rule are "pudding" and "garden"—by which, of course, James means Garden Party.

Another irony, for me at least, is that amongst the extraordinary repertoire of fine desserts—I confess a personal weakness—for which James became renowned, the two which got the most compliments, and seemed to give the greatest pleasure to our guests, were as English as you can get: summer pudding and Christmas pudding.

Bonne lecture!
Sir Peter Westmacott

James Viaene
A Life in Haute Cuisine

1937 Born in Crépy-en-Valois, the fifth in a family of eight children.

1951 Leaves school, aged thirteen and a half, to begin an apprenticeship with the patissier Monsieur Chaumard in Senlis.

1954 Continues his apprenticeship at the French Embassy in London …

1955 … and afterward with the Duke and Duchess of Windsor, with whom he stays, dividing his time between their residences in Paris and Gif-sur-Yvette, until 1960, with a break for military service in Algeria from 1957 to 1959.

1960 Completes his apprenticeship at the residence of the art dealer Georges Wildenstein.

1962 Now a chef, he enters the service of the Argentinian racehorse breeder Jean de Souza Lage.

1965 Becomes chef to Pierre Dupuy, owner of the *Petit Parisien* ….

1966 ... before leaving a year later to enter the service of the banker Michel David-Weill.

1970 Becomes chef at the British Ambassador's Residence in Paris, serving under ten ambassadors.

1972 Receives the Royal Victorian Medal from Queen Elizabeth II.

1979 Awarded the Médaille d'Or des Cuisiniers Français.

2000 James is made a Member of the Most Excellent Order of the British Empire (MBE).

Joins l'Académie Culinaire de France. **2003**

2005 Appointed Chevalier de l'Ordre du Mérite Agricole.

2010 Invested with the Légion d'honneur by Prime Minister François Fillon.

2011 Retires from the kitchens of the British Embassy, after forty years of faithful service.

$\mathcal{A}$ Return to Insouciance

"Are you really sure you want to be a chef? You must be mad! But if it's what you really want to do, then don't even think of getting married. The work and the hours are just incompatible with family life. It's a true vocation: no home life can stand the pressure." The year was 1954. Marcel Glé then reigned over the kitchens at the Hôtel de Marigny, Baron Alain de Rothschild's mansion, a mere stone's throw from the Elysée Palace, which was later to be acquired by the French state as accommodation for state visits. The great chef was quizzing a young man of seventeen, who had applied to be an apprentice in the kitchens of the French Embassy in London. It was a tough life, he warned him, but chefs for great private houses were highly sought after.

In the years after World War II, France yearned to live again and to forget about the war, with all its restrictions and privations. Entertaining had not stopped altogether during the Occupation. Marie-Laure de Noailles, one of the doyennes of Paris high society, continued to give dinners for close friends at her palatial residence on place des Etats-Unis, passing a plate round at the end of the meal for her guests to donate their ration tickets and the British Embassy in Paris, with Duff and Diana Cooper, remained one of Paris' most glittering salons. But it was after the Liberation that life in Paris really took off again—and in style.

Saint-Germain-des-Prés pulsated to the rhythms of jazz and swing, while the cafés of the Left Bank hosted a galaxy of talent including Jean-Paul Sartre, Simone de Beauvoir, Boris Vian, Jacques Prévert, and Juliette Gréco, to name but a few. In the world of high society, meanwhile, aristocrats, members of the *grande bourgeoisie*, and wealthy foreigners rubbed shoulders with artists, writers, and poets. Life was one long glittering round of lavish balls and parties, even more sumptuous than before the war.

The costume balls that had been all the rage in the 1920s now made their appearance again. The Marquis de Cuevas threw a Goya-themed ball, and Hélène Rochas revived *My Fair Lady* at the Grande Cascade in the Bois de Boulogne. And at the Palazzo Labia, his recently acquired Venetian residence, Charles de Bestegui, dressed for the occasion as a high official of the Venetian Republic, greeted his masked guests—a veritable who's who of the international jet set—as they stepped out of the gondolas in which they had floated along the Grand Canal toward the most lavish ball of the century.

In this newly rediscovered atmosphere of insouciance, the art of entertaining flourished once more. Marie-Blanche de Polignac, daughter of Jeanne Lanvin, invited artists and musicians including Francis Poulenc, Georges and Nora Auric, Arthur Rubinstein, and Pierre Barillet to her estate at Kerbastic in Brittany, where the fragrance of magnolia, jasmine, and wisteria wafted through the sheltered gardens. Her meticulously planned menus included not only the great classics, such as her

FACING PAGE *A dinner at the Hôtel Lambert, 1950.*

11

famous *soufflé aux oeufs pochés* (soufflé with poached eggs), but also more experimental dishes such as paella, then completely unknown in France and greeted by Denise Bourdon with dismay: "What sort of cuisine *is* this?" An enthusiastic reception for such foreign dishes was still a distant prospect. In the evening her chef, René Aupicon, would come to the drawing room to discuss the dishes he had prepared, to hear her suggestions, and to offer his own ideas.

At his Neuilly residence, meanwhile, the Chilean millionaire Arturo Lopez entertained in even more lavish style, throwing dinner parties for twenty or so guests at sumptuous tables laid with silver timbales, Sèvres porcelain, and gold from the collections of Catherine the Great. Paris high society also convened at the large dinner parties given by Louise de Vilmorin at Verrières, for which, aided by her faithful maid, she would herself prepare *les oeufs à la tripe*, the classic combination of hard-boiled eggs, onions, and Béchamel sauce that André Malraux adored. She was an exception, however. Society ladies of the period might devise menus and critique recipes, but, faced with a saucepan of water to boil they would have been completely at a loss.

In this privileged world, chefs were the key to successful entertaining. One simply had to have the best. Stealing was not unknown. Marie-Laure de Noailles boasted of having "kidnapped" the chef who worked for the Anchorenas, the wealthy Argentinian family who lived in immense style in their avenue Foch apartment with doors painted by Braque.

ABOVE *Cecil Beaton, Alexis de Redé, Daisy Fellowes, and Edward James at a ball at the Hôtel Lambert in 1950. Daisy Fellowes is wearing her famous "Hindu" necklace set with emeralds, sapphires, rubies, and diamonds ordered from Cartier in 1936.*
FACING PAGE *Alexis de Redé and Étienne de Beaumont at a ball at the Hôtel Lambert, 1950.*

Mr. and Mrs. Arturo Lopez-Willshaw,
Francine Weisweiller, Édouard Dermit,
and Jean Cocteau at the Château de Groussay, 1957.
Photograph taken at the Château de Versailles for
the French magazine L'Art et la mode, *December 1952.*

1

A CHEF'S VOCATION

$\mathcal{O}$nce Upon a Time...

IN ANGLO-SAXON COUNTRIES, FRIENDSHIPS HAVE ALWAYS TENDED TO BE SEALED BY A DRINK; IN FRANCE from as early as the fifteenth century, by contrast, the most pressing matters have been addressed over the dining table. Agnès Sorel, favorite of King Charles VII, was a pioneer in engaging the finest chefs to concoct salmis of woodcock and timbales in order to keep her royal lover firmly in her clutches. Three centuries later, Louis XV liked to serve sumptuously sophisticated dinners to two or three couples. To protect his guests' privacy, he even had an ingenious system installed whereby the dining table disappeared through the floor at the end of every course, winched down and up again, freshly laid, by unseen hands. Napoleon was happy with a couple of fried eggs served on an occasional table, but Cambacérès called him to order: "How do you expect to win friends if you do not offer them the best? It is around the table that you exert your influence over people, and good politics and good cuisine are to some degree indistinguishable from each other."

The chef's profession thus developed to serve the nobility, requiring no specific qualifications but a vast breadth of experience. Years of apprenticeship were needed to learn how to cook a large and recherché range of dishes, including terrines, fish, meats, sauces, and pastries, while also having the skills to run a kitchen and to be able to work alone, or to manage staff and train commis chefs (trainee chefs who learn about all the different aspects of cooking whilst working in a kitchen).

In the twentieth century, co-opted by their seniors in the profession, chefs began to form a sort of clan, the Mutuelle de France. At the beginning of *Les Trente Glorieuses*, France's three decades of post-war prosperity, there were still three hundred private chefs working in Paris (as opposed to four hundred in 1937 and just twenty today), all members of the Mutuelle, which found them positions in grand private houses. A handful of women, including Odette, chef to Pierre David-Weill, and Juliette, chef to Baron Thiery, also managed to find acceptance in this small and highly select band. But it was very much a man's world.

When the chef at the Hôtel de Marigny quizzed him in 1954, James Viaene was still dreaming of joining this gastronomic elite. Despite his very British-sounding first name, the young man was French, and had been brought up with his brother and six sisters by his mother and father, a cabinetmaker by trade, at Crépy-en-Valois. Family life was strict and frugal, but happy. As

PAGE 17 *James Viaene in his bedroom
at the French Embassy in London, c. 1954.*
FACING PAGE *The Duke and Duchess of Windsor's country
house in Gif-sur-Yvette, and James Viaene around
1955 when he entered their service as an apprentice.*

19

a child during World War II, he had watched his mother simmering many a pot-au-feu, the dish that for him was to become as evocative as Proust's madeleine. His outstanding singing voice earned him a place in the *Petits Chanteurs à la Croix de Bois*, the famous boys' choir, but the thing he loved most was making cakes. So, at the age of thirteen and a half, he left school without any qualifications (he would catch up later) to become an apprentice at the Chaumard patisserie in the Oise, holders of the secret recipe for the famous "senlisien," a honey biscuit that was the specialty of the town of Senlis. He worked there for three years: the first he spent buttering molds and scouring baking trays, and the second preparing Viennese pastries. In his third year he was at last given access to the marble slab on which the cakes were made.

He loved the work, and dreamed of climbing up the ranks. So the warnings given him by Alain de Rothschild's chef did not worry him in the least: he was prepared to work seven days a week if he had to. For him, obtaining a position as an apprentice in the kitchens of an embassy was just the start of an adventure. As it turned out, it was to be the beginning of a career that was to span no fewer than fifty-eight years (fifty as a chef) in some of the grandest houses in Paris. This distinguished career was to find its culmination at the British Embassy, which, at a time when the upper echelons of society were abandoning their formerly lavish ways in favor of an altogether simpler lifestyle, proved to be one of the last refuges of the grand traditions of French cuisine.

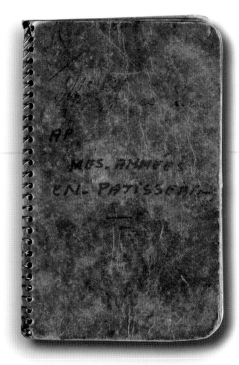
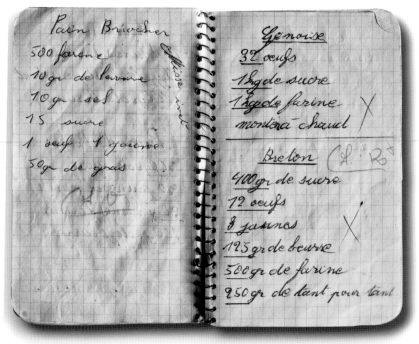

ABOVE *James Viaene's notebook, which he used during his apprenticeship at the Chaumard patisserie.*
FACING PAGE *A perfect English tea served in the opulent Empire setting of the Salon Jaune at the British Ambassador's Residence in Paris. George Hayter's portrait,* Antonio Canova, *painted in 1817, hangs next to the fireplace.*

Mother's Pot-au-Feu

CHILDHOOD MEMORIES

What could be simpler to make than a pot-au-feu? This great French family classic was a favorite of James's mother, who would leave it to simmer on the corner of the stove for her eight children. And yet it was a long time before James succeeded in penetrating the secrets of its success, and discovering once again the tastes of his childhood that were so deeply ingrained within him.

"Every morning at six o'clock, Mother would stoke the stove with coal. Then she would fill a large pot with water, put in some meat and marrowbones, and leave the pot on the stove to heat slowly. Later on, I understood how right she was to do it this way: if the meat cooks too quickly it goes hard, and can't release either the gelatin it contains, or the albumen that forms the froth on the surface. When the water came to the boil, she would move the pot to the side of the stove so that it reduced to a steady simmer, and skim off the froth. Then she would peel an onion, stud it with cloves, cut it in two, and place both halves on the stove until they turned a rich brown. After two hours of cooking, she would begin to add the herbs and seasonings, then the vegetables, freshly picked from the garden, one after another according to the time they took to cook. After four hours of this slow cooking, she would take the pot off the heat, explaining to me that as it cooled the meat would absorb the gelatin, the juices, and the vegetable flavors like a sponge, and this was what would give it all its flavor. And she was right, as the cooking had drawn everything out of the meat, and all that would be left otherwise were lumps of fiber with no taste. Mother would reheat her pot-au-feu and serve it cut into chunks, accompanied by potatoes boiled in the cooking stock. Father always got the bay leaf: Mother didn't do it on purpose, but it always made us all roar with laughter."

MOTHER'S POT-AU-FEU

My mother made her pot-au-feu not only as a delicious meal for us, but also as the basis for a good broth, which she would serve the next day with noodles and small pieces of stale bread—something she would never throw away.

Serves 10 or more

INGREDIENTS

2 ¼ lb. (1 kg) brisket	¾ lb. (300 g) turnips
1 lb. 2 oz. (500 g) round (USA), thick flank, or topside (UK)	6 medium leeks, whites only
1 lb. 2 oz. (500 g) shank (USA), clod, thick rib, or shin (UK)	1 celeriac root
(other pieces of meat such as beef cheeks, chuck,	1 green cabbage
or flanks are also suitable; just ask your butcher)	1 large bay leaf
1 lb. 2 oz. (500 g) marrow bones	2 sprigs thyme
1 large white or yellow onion, peeled	2 sprigs parsley
4 cloves	5 black peppercorns
1 garlic clove	Kosher salt
1 large celery stalk	Tomato sauce, kosher salt or fleur de sel,
1 ¼ lb. (600 g) carrots	and a few parsley leaves to garnish

Pour 6 ½ quarts (6 l) water into a large pot. Add the pieces of meat and the marrow bones. Bring slowly to a boil.

Peel the onion and stud it with the cloves. Peel the garlic clove. Wash the celery stalk and cut it into 2 ½-inch (7 cm) slices. Peel the carrots and turnips. Clean the leek whites. Peel the celeriac and quarter it. Remove the outer leaves of the cabbage and quarter it.

When the water is boiling, lower the heat so that it simmers gently. Skim. Add the onion, garlic clove, celery stalk, bay leaf, thyme, parsley, and peppercorns. Season with salt and cover the pot with the lid.

After 2 hours, add the carrots, leeks, and cabbage. One hour later, add the celeriac. Thirty minutes after that, add the turnips.

Cook for 4 hours altogether, remove from heat, and let cool. Skim off the fat that accumulates at the top of the broth.

To serve, reheat gently over low heat. Slice the meat and serve on a platter surrounded by the vegetables.

For a more modern version: Using individual pastry rings, place thin layers of the vegetables and meats in the rings and top with a slice of cooked marrow. Drizzle a little tomato sauce around the plate. Scatter a few grains of kosher salt on top and garnish with a parsley leaf. Remove the rings and bring to the table. Bon appétit! ❧

2 PARIS SOCIETY AT HOME

With the Duchess of Windsor

"SHE WAS GOOD TO US": SO JAMES VIAENE DESCRIBES HIS SECOND EMPLOYER, THE DUCHESS OF WINDSOR, with her reputation for being as severe, demanding, and harsh as she was elegant. In those few words he sums up the very particular relationship between the chef in a wealthy household and his employer, a combination of respect and proximity, of mutual dependence and gratitude, which ensured that the chef was genuinely part of the life of the family. Chefs were proud to be a part of these grand houses, whose distinguishing features were their French chef, English butler, and chauffeur-driven Rolls-Royce. They were ready to work up to seventy hours a week to cater for dinners in Paris, weekends in the country, and sometimes even vacations in the south of France, or to stay up all night making a birthday cake for the daughter of the house.

When he entered the Duke and Duchess of Windsor's service as an apprentice in 1955, James was eighteen years old, with a scooter, a head full of dreams, a hunger to learn—and a desire to enjoy himself. The chef, Monsieur Legros, soon left, to be replaced by Lucien Massy, one of the most respected, but also one of the most feared, chefs in Paris. This martinet wore a tie in the kitchen and always spoke in the third person. Nothing escaped him, he let nothing pass, and he terrorized his commis chefs, who spent their lives parroting *"oui chef"* at every order. Working alongside him were the butler, the footman Sidney, who had come from the Bahamas, three gardeners, several caretakers, and the couple (butler and maid) who looked after the Windsors' country house, the Moulin de la Tuilerie at Gif-sur-Yvette. A total of twenty-two staff worked in the duke and duchess's service. Under these circumstances, everything had to be just so.

Standards were of the very highest, and nothing less than excellence would do, either in Paris or in the country. The duchess was fierce in guarding her reputation as the best hostess in the world, bestowed upon her by the epicurean Edmond Bory. No detail escaped her notice. If she spotted a footman wearing red socks, she would draw it to the butler's attention the next day. On one occasion, when James had decorated a little foie gras canapé with two slices of truffle, she took the opportunity, when he came to present his menus for her inspection, as he did every morning, to remind him: "Last time you used three slices, it was more balanced."

Life in the mansion loaned to the Windsors by the French government, at Bagatelle on the edge of the Bois de Boulogne, combined the formality of the British court with the grand tradition of the aristocracy. Dinner consisted of small tables of six, the only number—in the duchess's view—that allowed conversation to flow and the food and wine to be properly appreciated (she would invariably ask how many bottles of wine had been drunk during the evening, as proof that her

FACING PAGE *The Duke and Duchess of Windsor at their home, rue de la Faisanderie, Paris, 1951.*

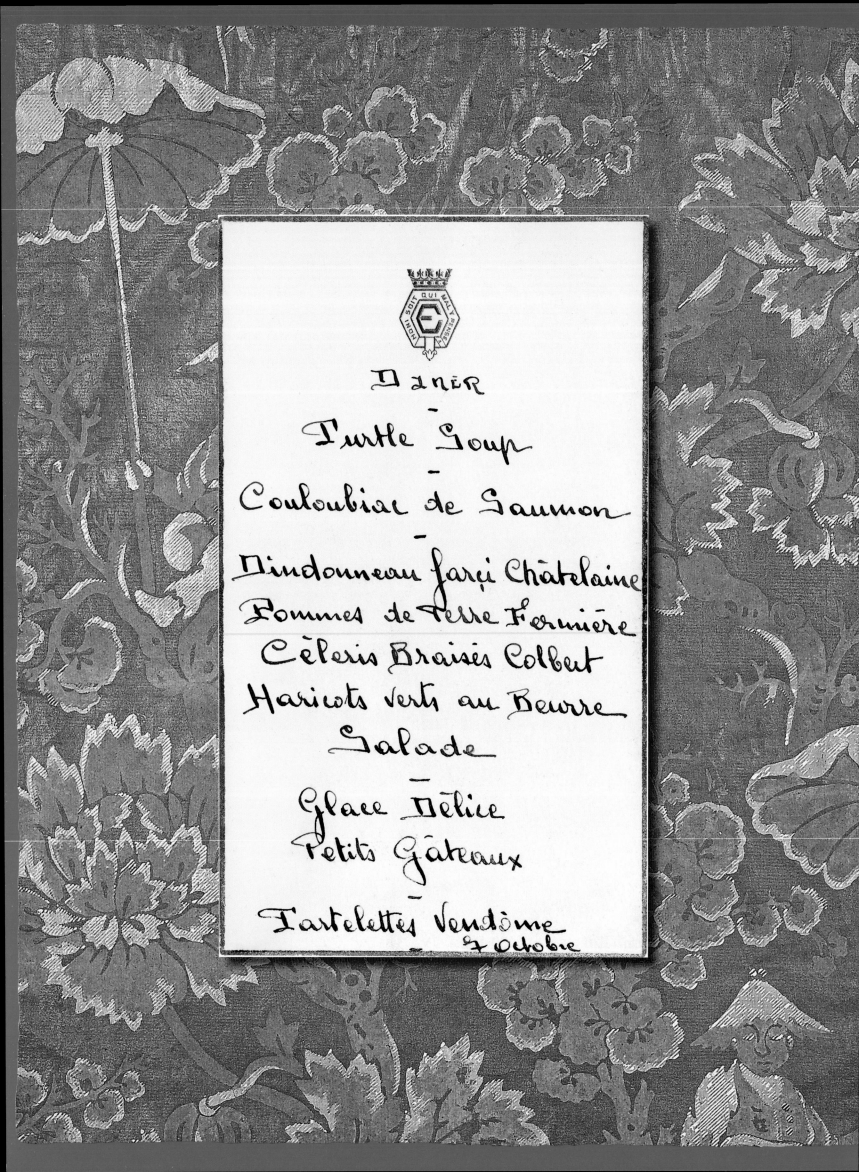

DINER
-
Turtle Soup
-
Couloubiac de Saumon
-
Dindonneau farci Châtelaine
Pommes de Terre Fermière
Céleris Braisés Colbert
Haricots verts au Beurre
Salade
-
Glace Délice
Petits Gâteaux
-
Tartelettes Vendôme
7 Octobre

guests had been relaxed and happy). The tables were laid with Sèvres porcelain by the nimble-fingered footman, Marcel Privé, and the menus featured the great classics—the duke was fond of lamb and poultry, especially braised chicken, his favorite dish. The Duchess, meanwhile, was partial to the parson's nose (the fatty point on the rump of cooked fowl), reputed to be rich in DNA. She liked vegetables in aspic, *consommé Trianon* topped with a spoonful of tomato granita with celery, and camembert marinated in white wine, served chilled. Ever watchful of her figure, whenever she went to her hairdresser, Alexandre, she would have a charming picnic basket brought to her, filled with delicacies such as chicken salad, green beans, and citrus fruit jelly.

On Friday evenings, the couple would draw up at Gif-sur-Yvette in their midnight-blue Cadillac, there to entertain a party of fifteen or so weekend guests. Naturally, the chef would come too. Etiquette was less formal than in Paris, but meticulous care was still devoted to every detail. As in most grand establishments at this time, breakfast was served to guests in their bedrooms. Each breakfast tray would be decked with fine linen and porcelain chosen to match the room's decorations, and was brought in—the ultimate refinement—by a maid whose uniform also coordinated with the color scheme, and who was therefore expected to change into a different colored uniform (pink, blue, yellow, or whatever) before entering each new room. At dinner the china was more rustic, with soup served in porcelain cabbage-shaped bowls. And the afternoon was spent playing cards, sipping champagne, and nibbling at small beef, ham, or chicken (but never cucumber) sandwiches.

The two absolute rules of the house were the twin requirements for the highest standards of refinement and rigor in every detail. While the Duchess was a stickler for protocol, the duke ventured to attempt one or two timid departures from the rules. He liked to put on his boots to go and check on new plantings with the gardeners, or to leave the plush limousines in the garage and go for a drive in one of the Citröen 2CVs. When the Tour de France passed through the village, he went to join members of staff on a hillock to watch the cyclists race past. And now and again he would wander through the garage and eye up James's scooter, though he was never bold enough to take it out for a spin.

Though customarily something of a martinet, the Duchess could also be surprising. When one of the commis chefs misjudged a bend while driving a 2CV from the Windsor fleet, ploughed into one of the glasshouses, and wrote off the car, she merely remarked that French cars were very flimsy. And she could be generous. On Christmas Eve every year, she would hire an outside chauffeur and hand the house over to the staff for them to enjoy their Christmas Eve dinner, complete with turkey, *bûches de Noël*, the traditional Christmas dessert served in France (never Christmas pudding, which was too British), wines from the duke's cellars, and cigars bought by him as a gift. The evening would close with a tombola, with lots drawn out of a hat for all the gifts—trinkets and objects in gold or semi-precious stones—that the Windsors had received over the previous year.

James is convinced that the Duchess wanted everyone in her household to be happy. And her staff were attached to her in return. When she left on her annual trip to the Waldorf Astoria in New York, the butler would always present her with a white orchid on the station platform, on behalf of her twenty-two employees. She would keep it with her in the train until Le Havre, and afterward in her cabin on board ship.

FACING PAGE *Menu of a dinner hosted by the Duke and Duchess of Windsor, c. 1955.*

ABOVE *The residence of the Duke and Duchess of Windsor located 4, route du Champ d'Entraînement, Neuilly-sur-Seine, France. The nineteenth-century villa, owned by the city of Paris, was leased to the couple from 1952 to 1986.*
FACING PAGE *The Duke of Windsor, July 11, 1960.*

FACING PAGE *The luxurious dining room
at 24, boulevard Suchet, first Parisian home
of the Duke and Duchess of Windsor.*
ABOVE *A view showing the exterior of the house.
The duke and duchess lived here between
1939 and 1949.*

35

LOBSTER MOUSSE

WITH SAUCE LIBÉRALE

Serves 6

INGREDIENTS

3 lobsters, about 1 ¼ lb. (600 g) apiece	1 tablespoon tomato paste
14 oz. (400 g) tomatoes	1 cup (250 ml) dry white wine
1 large shallot	7 sheets gelatin
3 tablespoons (40 g) butter	1 cup (250 ml) heavy cream
1 tablespoon olive oil	(whipping cream)
Piment d'Espelette (or Cayenne pepper)	Salt
	Freshly ground pepper

For the court-bouillon

14 oz. (400 g) carrots	Scant ½ cup (100 ml)
¾ lb. (300 g) onions	wine vinegar
1 sprig thyme	4 tablespoons (60 g) salt
1 bay leaf	10 black peppercorns

For the sauce

4 tablespoons (60 ml) mayonnaise	
2 tablespoons lobster sauce	
1 tablespoon cognac	

For the garnish

6 edible nasturtiums	
1 sprig of dill	

For the court-bouillon: Peel and slice the carrots. Peel and slice the onions into rounds. Pour 6 ½ quarts (6 l) into a large pot. Add the carrots, onions, thyme, bay leaf, vinegar, and salt. Bring to a boil. After 10 minutes, add the peppercorns and the lobsters. Simmer for 5 minutes. Remove from heat and let cool slowly.

Dip the tomatoes in boiling water for 10 seconds and refresh them briefly under cold water. Peel them, remove the seeds, and chop them. Peel the shallot and chop it.

Drain the lobsters. Extract the flesh from the tail and front claws. Remove the gravel sac from the head and discard it. If there is any coral roe, remove it and set aside for the sauce. Remove the flesh from the other claws. With a large knife, chop the flesh and the contents of the head.

For the mousse: In a small saucepan, melt the butter with the oil and lightly sauté the shallot. Add the chopped flesh from the head and claws and a pinch of *piment d'Espelette*. Sauté until nicely browned. Add the chopped tomato, tomato paste, white wine, and 1 cup (250 ml) of court-bouillon. Simmer gently for 20 minutes.

Soften the gelatin in a bowl of cold water. Adjust the seasoning of the sauce and strain through a fine-mesh sieve. Squeeze the water from the gelatin sheets and mix into the sauce until completely dissolved. Let cool in a mixing bowl. Lightly whip the cream and fold it in.

Line small ramekins with parchment paper. Divide the mixture among the ramekins and chill for at least 2 hours.

For the sauce: Crush the roe until smooth. Stir it into the mayonnaise with the lobster sauce and cognac.

To serve, turn the mousses out onto plates. Slice the lobster tails. On one side of the mousse, place a lobster claw and, on the other, the slices of half a tail. Garnish with a nasturtium, a small sprig of dill, and a little sauce. Serve this appetizer with a cucumber sambale (a spicy condiment used especially in Indonesia and Malaysia, made with chili peppers and other ingredients, such as sugar or coconut) and Melba toast.

You can also make this dish with crayfish or prawns. ❧

Dîner
~
Crême d'Asperges
~
Mousse de Homard froide
Sauce Libérale
Salade Concombres à la Crême
~
Poularde farcie Grimaldy
Petits Pois au Beurre
~
Sorbet aux Fraises
Petits Gâteaux
~
Tartelettes Vendôme
~
22 Mai 1956

FILLET OF BEEF WITH PÉRIGORD TRUFFLE PASTRY TRIANGLES

CARAMELIZED CARROTS, BRAISED LETTUCE, AND PEAS *À L'ANCIENNE*

Serves 8

INGREDIENTS

8 truffles, *Tuber melanosporum* if possible, 1 oz. (30 g) apiece
1 small carrot
1 medium onion
3 ½ tablespoons (50 g) butter
3 ¼ lb. (1.5 kg) beef fillet (not a thick one), trimmings reserved
1 bay leaf
1 tablespoon cornstarch

2 cups (500 ml) veal stock
1 lobe fresh duck foie gras
2 ¼ lb. (1 kg) puff pastry
1 egg yolk
1 tablespoon milk
¾ cup (200 ml) thick crème fraîche
Scant ½ cup (100 ml) port
Salt
Freshly ground pepper

For the garnish

3 lb. (1.3 kg) round carrots, or carrots cut into ovals
1 ¾ sticks (210 g) butter, divided
4 pinches sugar, divided
2 large lettuces, or 4 small ones, depending on the season
Veal stock as needed
3 lb. (1.3 kg) garden peas

16 pearl onions
1 small carrot
1 teaspoon flour
4 small, thin slices smoked bacon
½ tablespoon peanut oil
1 bunch watercress

For the base

1 slice sandwich loaf, just over 1 inch (3 cm) thick,
cut lengthwise to the length of the fillet
Oil for frying

Preheat the oven to 375°F (190°C). Peel the truffles and reserve the trimmings. Peel the carrot and slice it thickly. Peel the onion and cut it into small dice.

Melt 3 ½ tablespoons (50 g) butter in a flameproof roasting pan or large pot. Brown the beef on all sides for 5 minutes with the trimmings, carrot, and onion. Add the bay leaf. Roast for 15 minutes, turning the meat every 5 minutes. Remove the beef from the pot and season it all over with salt. Wrap it in parchment paper and keep in a warm place. Do not clean the pan, as you will need the juices for the next step.

Dissolve the cornstarch in the veal stock. Pour it into the roasting pan and simmer gently for 20 minutes.

Strain the liquid through a fine-mesh sieve into a small saucepan. Add the truffle peel, cover with a lid, and let infuse.

Remove the membrane from the foie gras and slice it finely. Remove the veins and season with salt and pepper. Heat a frying pan over high heat without adding any fat and sear the foie gras. Chop it finely. Let it cool, otherwise it will melt the butter in the puff pastry when spread over it.

Roll the puff pastry to a thickness of just under ⅛ inch (2 mm) and, with a cookie cutter or glass, cut out eight 2 ¼-inch (6 cm) rounds. Brush them with a little water. Coat a truffle in the chopped foie gras and place it into the center of the pastry. Repeat with the remaining seven rounds.

Fold the pastry rounds into triangle shapes and press down firmly round the edges to seal. Combine the egg yolk with the milk and brush the tops of the triangles. Let rest for 5 minutes. Increase the oven temperature to 400°F (200°C) and bake for 10 minutes at the most, keeping a careful eye on how the triangles color. They should not be too dark.

For the garnish: Prepare the carrots: Peel them and place them in a sauté pan with 5 ½ tablespoons (80 g) butter and 2 pinches sugar. Pour in just enough salted water to cover them and cook, uncovered, for about 20 minutes until almost all the water has evaporated. There should be a syrupy liquid at the bottom of the pan to make the carrots shiny. Keep warm.

Carefully wash the lettuce. Tie them up with kitchen twine so they remain closed. Cook them for 5 minutes in a large volume of boiling salted water. Drain, untie the twine, and cut lengthwise. If you have large lettuces, cut them into quarters; if you have small ones, cut them into halves.

Fold the pieces over three times. Butter a sauté pan with 3 ½ tablespoons (50 g) butter. Place the lettuce pieces around the pan. Pour in enough veal stock to cover them and season with pepper. Cover with a disk of parchment paper in which you have made a small hole in the center. Cook until all the liquid has evaporated and keep warm.

Shell the peas. Peel the onions. Peel and slice the carrot. Combine the flour with 5 ½ tablespoons (80 g) butter. Place all these ingredients in a pot with ¾ cup (200 ml) water, 2 pinches sugar, and 1 pinch salt. Cover with the lid and simmer gently over low heat for about 15 minutes, until the vegetables are done—they should retain some crunch. Keep warm.

In a small sauté pan, cook the slices of bacon in the peanut oil until they are very dry. Drain them on paper towel to remove any excess fat and break them into small pieces.

To make the base, pour oil 1 ½ inches (4 cm) deep into a large frying pan and heat. With a small knife, make small zigzags around the slice of bread. Fry it until golden on both sides and drain on paper towel.

Strain the sauce to remove the truffle peel. Stir in the crème fraîche and port. As you reheat gently, process the sauce with an immersion blender until it is foamy.

Place the bread base on the serving platter. Slice the fillet of beef and carefully arrange the slices on the bread. Arrange the lettuce pieces, glazed carrots, and truffle pastry triangles around, alternating them. At one end of the platter, place the bunch of watercress. Transfer the peas to a vegetable dish and scatter them with the bacon bits. Pour the sauce into a sauce dish and serve. ❧

$\mathcal{I}$nterpreting the Masters' Recipes

"DURING MY TIME WITH THE DUCHESS OF WINDSOR I LEARNED A GREAT DEAL," JAMES RECALLS, "BUT IT was Georges Wildenstein's chef, Roger Harmand, who really opened my eyes." In order to take his training to a higher level and advance his apprenticeship, James entered the household of the art dealer Georges Wildenstein in 1960. Roger Harmand had learned his métier in the establishments of Cécile de Rothschild and the Princesse de Faucigny-Lucinge, and he was a pioneer in his field. In a world that was still deeply in thrall to the past, Harmand was an innovator. The recipes served at this time were exclusively those of the great masters of cuisine, such as Antonin Carême, Auguste Escoffier, and Curnonsky (the celebrated writer on gastronomy). Chefs would follow their methods to the letter, but as the quantities of ingredients were often not given, and the cooking varied according to the heat of the hob (generally wood-fired) and the oven, they would produce very different results. Chefs were judged according to their way with the great classics, and employers—always looking for familiar flavors and tastes from their childhood—were severe. Georges Wildenstein had abiding memories of the Alsatian kouglof of his early years, for instance. He ordered all his chefs to make it and was never satisfied with the results, invariably judging them too dense, too sweet, too heavy on raisins, or whatever. Only a young commis chef called James, who had started his working life with a pastry chef, contrived to produce the perfect light texture, an achievement that earned him the considerable surprise of seeing his employer come into the kitchen to congratulate him, for the first and only time. Compliments were rare. When he ordered an orange sorbet, Georges Wildenstein detested seeing it garnished with orange (had he asked for a fruit salad?) and when he asked for a foie gras salad he would allow a few truffles with it but never lobster, as this would be too much.

Yet Wildenstein's chef, Roger Harmand, was the first to experiment with new methods. Take the cooking of trout *au bleu*, for instance. In the Duchess of Windsor's kitchen, the chef would gut the live fish and plunge them into the water one after the other, gauging their freshness as they turned blue in the pot. Roger Harmand, by contrast, would stun the fish and sprinkle their skin with a few drops of vinegar to turn them blue, so that he could reserve them in a dish and plunge them all together into the boiling water, where they would cook for the same length of time. Handy and practical. Harmand would garnish a braised gigot of lamb in the most imaginative and unexpected ways, and conjure delicious petits fours out of improbable combinations of leftover puff pastry and rich shortcrust pastry. "Be creative, trust your own ideas," he would urge his commis chefs. "People may criticize, but it will give you pleasure and satisfaction." This was a novel approach for the 1960s, heralding changes to come.

FACING PAGE *Chef James preparing his sea bass braised in champagne (see page 128).*

44

Family Mealtimes chez Wildenstein

In the early 1960s, when "le Tout-Paris" was busy partying, James was completing his apprenticeship at the Wildensteins'. Life in their Paris Mansion on rue de la Boétie still revolved around the family. Or more particularly around grandfather Georges (son of the founder of this dynasty of art dealers and a man respected by all), his son Daniel, and his two grandsons Alec and Guy. The Wildenstein clan lived in lavish style, with a stable of racehorses, walls hung with masterpieces, and a superior Rolls Royce parked outside the mansion, tended by a chauffeur who regularly flicked its gleaming bodywork with a feather duster. Yet there was very little entertaining on a grand scale, or indeed none at all: lunches were small and private, with just a single guest, while dinner was very often a family occasion. At table, a book containing the chef's menu suggestions would be passed round for everyone to add their own suggestions and preferences. Then Georges Wildenstein would invariably cross them all out again, and demand instead fillets of sole with braised vegetables (his favorite was crosnes, or Chinese artichokes) and tinned petits pois (he disliked the fresh variety), followed by sorbets or rice pudding. The menu for Sunday evening—the chef's day off—was set in stone: smoked tongue from Goldenberg, the Jewish deli on avenue de Wagram, with horseradish and vegetables.

47

FILLET OF SOLE MURAT

Serves 8

INGREDIENTS

Fillets of 4 large soles, about 1 lb. 2 oz. (500 g) apiece, skin removed

4 cups (1 l) milk

1 ¼ lb. (600 g) potatoes

8 cooked artichoke bottoms

8 small plum tomatoes

5 tablespoons (70 g) butter

1 tablespoon oil

Flour to dust the fillets

Salt

Freshly ground pepper

Juice of 1 large lemon and chopped flat-leaf parsley to garnish

Cut the sole fillets into finger-wide strips and soak them in the milk.

Peel the potatoes and cut into very small cubes. Cut the artichoke bottoms into 8.

Drop the tomatoes into boiling water for 30 seconds. Refresh, drain, and peel them. Cut them into halves lengthwise and season with salt. Place downward on paper towel so that they exude their liquid.

Season the artichoke bottoms with salt and sauté them in 1 ½ tablespoons (20 g) butter. Season the potato cubes with salt and sauté them in 1 ½ tablespoons (20 g) butter until golden. Cook the tomatoes in a pan with the oil. Keep the vegetables warm.

Drain the strips of sole and pat them dry with paper towel or a cloth. Season them with salt and dust them with flour. In a skillet over high heat, melt 2 tablespoons (30 g) butter and, when it is sizzling, cook the fish for 1 minute maximum. Be careful not to overcook as it will become dry.

Arrange the fish, artichoke pieces, and potato cubes on a serving platter and combine carefully. Season lightly with pepper. Surround with tomatoes, drizzle with lemon juice, and sprinkle with parsley.

You can also drizzle with a little meat jus or glaze.

I prefer to shape the potatoes into mini French fries and fry them until they are very crisp. I then combine them with the other vegetables at the last minute.

If you use raw artichokes, the simplest way to prepare them is to boil them, remove the leaves (which you can eat with a vinaigrette), and then use the bottoms. ❧

A Chef's First Steps

AFTER THREE YEARS WORKING IN PATISSERIE AND SIX YEARS AS AN APPRENTICE, THE TIME HAD COME TO MOVE on and up. In 1962, therefore, it was as chef that James entered the household of Jean de Souza Lage, an Argentinian racehorse owner with a Brazilian wife. This consummate gentleman, who would raise his hat to his gardener, lived in lavish style at Wood Lodge, near Chantilly, where life was one long round of dinners small and large, lunches, and receptions for six, ten, twenty, or thirty guests, in addition to the buffet lunch that his employer always gave before the Prix de Diane, one of France's most elegant horse-racing events. The challenge was all the greater as Jean de Souza Lage was a member of the Club des Cent, the highly select circle of one hundred of France's most distinguished gourmets, all of them great aficionados, and above all connoisseurs, of fine cuisine. These were not diners who could be fooled by the usual tricks of the trade, such as fixing a sauce by adding a little too much cream; these were discerning palates able to appreciate a perfect harmony of ingredients and flavorings, or to detect a lack of it. As they explained: "When someone says, 'Hmm, that tastes of cloves,' it means that the flavor of cloves is far too strong. When they say, 'Do I taste cloves?', it means it is a little too strong. But when they say, 'What's that subtle flavor? I must pin it down,' it means it is just right."

Offering new experiences and surprises that would also meet the exacting standards of these éminences grises of the world of gastronomy was a seemingly impossible challenge, but one to which James was prepared to rise. In a well-to-do household such as this, he was fully aware that he had to know how to prepare a wide variety of dishes and menus, from turbot to fillet of beef and noisettes of venison to partridge salad, not forgetting desserts, the all-important final note and lingering last memory of any meal.

Adapting to the different ways and idiosyncrasies of each new household and taking them all in your stride, without betraying any hint of surprise, is a subtle art. Every family has its own particular habits and favorite dishes, with which a new chef may be unfamiliar. Baron Elie de Rothschild's table was famous for its celebrated *soufflé Rothschild*, a delicacy that, contrary to general belief, was not made with dried fruit, but rather consisted of two halves cooked on both sides in a frying pan and sandwiched together with apricot purée. The Baron's aunt, Baroness Edouard de Rothschild, used to offer her guests a variation that was cooked in the oven without a mold. And Pierre Dupuy, owner of *Le Petit Parisien*, liked to serve thick slices of Pauillac lamb, carved from a gigot roasted over vine shoots to give it an outstanding flavor.

Meals at Chantilly had an unusual Brazilian and Argentinian flavor, as favored by the mistress of the house, including dishes such as *fechuada*, little black beans with dried beef, and manioc couscous with fish. "I'd never heard of them, but I knuckled down," James remembers. "When you become a

FACING PAGE *Wood Lodge, Jean de Souza Lage's property near Chantilly, France.*

chef, you are thrown into a household that is completely unfamiliar to you, and you have to adapt." He had to adapt again when he joined the service of another member of the Club des Cent, Michel David-Weill. The chairman of the Lazard Frères investment bank and his wife, Mme David-Weil, also did a great deal of entertaining, both at their Paris residence on rue Saint-Guillaume and at their country house in the south of France, where they welcomed family friends. Hélène oversaw every last detail. She did not just employ James as a chef, but she also had frequent meetings with him to discuss recipes, to tell him what she liked or otherwise, and to ask his views. For the David-Weills, there had to be a perfect harmony in every aspect of the occasion: in the flavors of the dishes, their presentation, the china, and the service. In their view, mealtimes were when the day was put on hold, when everything stopped for a few moments of pleasure and enjoyment.

Tastes in the David-Weill household were traditional, with favored dishes including roast chicken and *blanquette de veau* with rum baba for dessert. In the south of France, they often served *chaud-froid de poulet*, a dish invented by chance one day when an impatient employer asked out of the blue for something to eat, urgently, and the chef got out some cold cooked chicken coated in a white sauce that had set in the refrigerator.

In all these grand residences, James had constantly to juggle and improvise in the face of the unexpected. Were there to be ten guests, or twenty, or even thirty? The great thing was always to have enough to hand, while never letting anything go to waste. Nothing was thrown away, and leftovers were always recycled in *parmentiers* (shepherd's pie) or little sandwiches.

From his vantage point in the kitchen James loved this life, with all its mad rushes, its stresses and strains, and its requirements for perfection and constant pleasure. But by the late 1960s, this way of life was starting to disappear.

ABOVE *A sitting room in Wood Lodge.*
FACING PAGE *Jean de Souza Lage dancing with his mother,*
Dulce de Martinez de Hoz, in 1959.

53

Luncheon at the Prix de Diane

A hard-boiled egg soufflé as a supporting act to the Prix de Diane? Well, why not? In the 1960s, as the prelude to the legendary horse race for three-year-old thoroughbred fillies, run at Chantilly since 1843, Jean de Souza Lage would host an annual luncheon in mid-June at his Chantilly residence. Chef James's cold mousse was to become one of the signature dishes at these glittering occasions—for if the Argentine racehorse owner never carried off the prize, his parties were nevertheless one of the highlights of the Paris season.

Some fifty guests would gather on the terrace, which would be dotted with small tables set for eight. There the crème de la crème of Paris society would rub shoulders with representatives of prominent families in the racing world, and with South American compatriots of the host, whose close friends included the Fels, Waldners, Bembergs, and Carcanos.

On the menu would be cold appetizers and barbecued whole lamb, basted for several days in a marinade of lemon juice, olive oil, thyme, and bay leaves until the flesh was almost white. For dessert there were meringues glacées *and fruit with* confiture de lait, *a thick caramel sauce. Altogether, this was an alfresco lunch that combined the ultimate in elegance with apparently artless simplicity. It was James's job to carve the lamb, a responsibility the diffident young chef—who would far rather have been in his kitchen—approached with some trepidation. Jean de Souza Lage's luncheons gave way years ago to a chic picnic and hat contest conceived by Hermès, sponsors of the race for nearly a quarter of a century. The prize goes to the most devastating, spectacular, or eccentric headgear, in homage to the Belle Epoque, when no respectable society lady would dream of going to the races bareheaded.*

Times and conventions have changed. But the Prix de Diane is one of the last remaining events of the Paris season at which an elegant turnout remains de rigueur. *And a little of that elegance will rub off on any alfresco summer lunch or dinner that features* Soufflé aux œufs durs *on its menu.*

ABOVE *Prince Ali Khan with Duff Cooper, former*
British Ambassador to France, at the Prix de Diane, June 6, 1949.
FACING PAGE *Baron Guy and Baroness Marie-Hélène de Rothschild*
with their horse, Cerisoles, after winning the Prix de Diane,
June 5, 1960.

HARD-BOILED EGG SOUFFLÉ

I created this soufflé while working for Monsieur Jean and Madame Philomène de Souza Lage. Monsieur de Souza Lage was from Argentina and his wife from Brazil. I used Parmesan cheese the first time I made it. After that, I used Roquefort, Gruyère, Stilton, Cheddar, and even sometimes a combination of these cheeses.

Prepare a day ahead

Serves 9 to 10

INGREDIENTS

4 sheets gelatin, or 1 ¾ teaspoons powdered gelatin	1 heaping tablespoon chopped chives
1 ½ tablespoons (20 g) butter	1 heaping tablespoon chopped tarragon
2 tablespoons (20 g) flour	7 oz. (200 g) grated Parmesan
1 ¼ cups (300 ml) milk	*Piment d'Espelette*
6 hard-boiled eggs	Salt
1 anchovy fillet	Fresh herbs and chopped hard-boiled eggs to garnish
2 cups (500 ml) heavy cream (whipping cream)	

SPECIAL EQUIPMENT

A soufflé mold, diameter 6 inches (15 cm) and depth 2 ½ to 3 inches (7 to 8 cm) and a strip of parchment paper 24 × 4 inches (60 × 11 cm).

Soften the gelatin sheets in cold water, or dissolve the powder in 1 tablespoon (15 ml) water. Line the sides of the soufflé mold with the strip of parchment paper. Use twine or two elastic bands to keep it in place at the top and the bottom, and secure the ends with a paper clip or staple.

In a small heavy-bottomed saucepan, melt the butter. Add the flour and stir with a small whisk or wooden spoon for 1 minute. Gradually pour in the milk, stirring continuously, and bring to a boil. Let simmer gently, still stirring, for 1 minute.

Squeeze the water from the gelatin sheets and add to the sauce. Mix in until completely dissolved then remove from heat. Pour into a mixing bowl and let cool.

Shell the hard-boiled eggs and chop them roughly. With a knife, chop the anchovy fillet. Whip the cream.

Add the eggs, anchovy, chives, tarragon, grated Parmesan, and 2 pinches *piment d'Espelette* to the cooled béchamel. Carefully fold in the whipped cream. Check the seasoning.

Pour the mixture into the soufflé mold and chill for at least 12 hours, until firm.

The next day, garnish the soufflé with fresh herbs and chopped hard-boiled eggs.

To serve, run the blade of a small knife between the soufflé and the parchment paper. Remove the twine or elastic bands, and then carefully take off the parchment paper. Place the soufflé on a large plate or a dish covered with a napkin. Surround with lettuce or watercress leaves. ❧

ICED SAINT JAMES CAKE

I made this dessert for the first time for the Prix de Diane horse race. It comprises different flavored ice creams or sorbets and rounds of meringue. I served it with dulce de leche, known in France as confiture de lait. *In summer, I always make fruit ice creams; in winter, I prefer vanilla, coffee, chocolate, praline, and other classic flavors.*

Serves 8

INGREDIENTS

For the meringue

8 egg whites	1 heaped teaspoon cornstarch
1 heaped teaspoon granulated sugar	1 teaspoon lemon juice
3 cups plus 1 scant cup (1 lb. 2 oz./500 g) confectioners' sugar	

For the ice creams

4 cups (1 l) whole milk	1 ¼ cups (300 ml) puréed strawberries
½ vanilla bean, slit lengthwise	5 oz. (150 g) shelled pistachios
1 ¼ cups (9 oz., 250 g) sugar	1 tablespoon granulated sugar
12 egg yolks	

For the dulce de leche

4 cups (1 l) whole milk
2 ⅔ cups (1 lb. 2 oz./500 g) light brown sugar*
1 vanilla bean, slit lengthwise

SPECIAL EQUIPMENT
A mold, diameter 6 inches (15 cm), depth at least 4 inches (10 cm).

For the dulce de leche: Gently simmer the milk with the light brown sugar and vanilla, stirring from time to time, for about 2 hours, until it has thickened and become a light caramel in color. Let cool.

For the meringues: Preheat the oven to 195°F (90°C). Butter and flour a baking sheet. With the rim of a mold just slightly smaller than the 6-inch (15 cm) mold used to make the dessert, trace four circles on the sheet. They should be 5 ½ inches (14 cm) in diameter.

Beat the egg whites with the granulated sugar until firm peaks form. Combine the confectioners' sugar with the cornstarch. With a flexible spatula, carefully fold the confectioners' sugar-cornstarch mixture into the egg whites. At this point, I always add the lemon juice, which prevents the meringue from coloring too much. Spread the meringue in the circles traced on the baking sheet, ensuring that the thickness is ⅕ inch (5 mm). Place the sheet in the oven, jamming a small rolled-up piece of paper into the door so that it is about 1 inch (2 cm) ajar. This allows the steam to escape. At this low temperature, baking is slow—about 3 hours—but the meringues do not color too much. When they are done, store in an airtight container.

For the ice creams: To make the custard, bring the milk to a boil with the vanilla bean. In a large mixing bowl, beat the sugar with the egg yolks until thick, pale, and creamy. Pour the milk over the mixture, continuing to beat. Return the liquid to the saucepan and stir continuously until it thickens. Do not allow to boil. As soon as it reaches the desired texture, remove from heat and place the bottom of the saucepan in cold water to stop it from cooking further. Continue to stir until completely cooled.

Strain the custard through a fine-mesh sieve and divide it into three. Leave one third vanilla flavored. Stir the puréed strawberries into the second third of the custard until thoroughly combined. For the third flavor, blend the pistachios with the water and sugar until the mixture is a creamy texture. Stir it into the last third of the custard until thoroughly combined. Place in an ice cream maker and follow the manufacturer's directions. If you don't have an ice cream maker, pour the three mixtures into seperate bowls and freeze, stirring from time to time, until they reach the consistency of ice cream. If you are using an ice cream maker that needs to be re-frozen after each use, keep the other mixtures well chilled in the refrigerator. They will keep for up to two days.

To assemble the dessert, place a disk of meringue at the bottom of the mold. Flatten one of the ice creams over it. Place another meringue disk over the ice cream and then another meringue disk. Spread the last ice cream over the meringue and top with the last meringue disk. Place the mold in the freezer.

If the meringue disks are slightly larger than the inside of the mold, cut them by placing a lid or plate of the right diameter over them and saw them carefully with a serrated knife.

To turn the dessert out of the mold, run a small knife around the inside of the mold. Place a serving platter over the top and turn out the dessert onto it. Drizzle a little dulce de leche around it.

Garnish as you please. I prefer sliced almonds that I roast with a little sugar to caramelize. Serve the remaining dulce de leche in a sauce dish. Use a serrated knife to cut the dessert into portions. ❧

* Light brown sugar gives the best taste to dulce de leche.

Entertaining chez the David-Weills

*Where can the art of entertainment—with that instinctive elegance
and refinement that now seem part of a lost world—still be found?
At the Paris residence of Hélène David-Weill, the wife of Michel David-Weill
(last descendant of the family that founded the banking firm Lazard),
who is a patron and collector of the arts, and was for many
years President of the Union centrale des Arts décoratifs.
"People say Paris society doesn't exist any more. It does," she declares,
"but it is discreet. Paris has lost its aura. In London and New York people still
get dressed up, but not in Paris. Wearing a tie is viewed as fuddy-duddy now.
Women no longer come from all over the world for the couture collections. Paris
is no longer the world's only artistic center, and travel has displaced
the rituals of Paris society as a form of distraction." Yet there are still some
grand houses where tradition lives on. And the David-Weill residence is one
of them. Mealtimes are moments in the day when everything pauses,
and you are encouraged to set aside the preoccupations of life in order
to share a convivial occasion with others. These special moments should be
preserved by every means possible. And everyone can do it in their own way,
according to their own tastes and means. The David-Weills alternate
luncheons with intimate suppers and with grand dinners, which offer an
opportunity for a slightly "bolder" approach to guest lists and seating plans.
Every detail is imbued with excellence, from objets d'art and paintings
on the walls to table settings and services. Menus are both traditional
and impeccable, in the image of the mistress of house, featuring her favorite*
grenadins de veau, chaud-froid de poulet, *and Waldorf salad, followed by*
mille-feuille *and rum baba. The very epitome of entertaining in style.*

65

Veal Fillet with Mushroom Duxelles

Braised Belgian endives, French beans, and Vichy carrots

Serves 8

INGREDIENTS

1 small onion (2 oz./50 g)	1 ⅔ cups (400 ml) dry white wine
1 medium carrot (3 oz./80 g)	Veal stock as needed
2 ½ inches (6 cm) celery stalk	Scant ½ cup (100 ml) Madeira
4 tablespoons (60 g) butter	Salt
16 veal medallions from the fillet	Freshly ground pepper
Flour for dusting	
1 small *bouquet garni* (parsley, thyme, and bay leaf)	

For the mushroom duxelles

1 large shallot	1 heaping tablespoon thick crème fraîche
1 lb. 2oz. (500 g) button mushrooms, white or crimini	1 small truffle
1 tablespoon tomato paste	Freshly ground pepper

For the Vichy carrots

3 ¼ lb. (1.5 kg) carrots	1 bottle (1.25 l) Vichy water or other seltzer water,
3 ½ tablespoons (50 g) butter	or 5 cups water and the juice of half a lemon
3 tablespoons (35 g) sugar	1 tablespoon chopped parsley

Peel the onion and the carrot. Cut the onion, carrot, and celery stalk into fine dice. Sauté them with 2 tablespoons (30 g) butter until nicely browned. Set aside.

Season the veal medallions with salt and pepper. Dip them in flour, patting them well so that they are well coated (this will bind the sauce). Heat the remaining butter in a sauté pan large enough to contain the fillets and place them side by side to brown well. Add the diced vegetables, the bouquet garni, and the white wine. Pour in the veal stock until the meat is just covered. Bring to a boil, cover with the lid, and simmer very gently for 1 ½ hours, turning the fillets at least four times while they cook.

While the meat is cooking, prepare the Vichy carrots: Peel the carrots and slice them finely. Place them in a sauté pan with the butter, sugar, water, and a little salt. Bring to a boil and cook over high heat until all the liquid has evaporated.

For the mushroom duxelles: Peel and chop the shallot. Clean the mushrooms and dice them finely. Heat the butter and sauté the mushrooms with the shallot. Stir in the tomato paste. Simmer for 2 to 3 minutes. Finely dice the truffle. Add the crème fraîche and diced truffle. Season with salt and pepper.

Remove the veal fillets and keep them warm. Remove the *bouquet garni* from the pan and bring the liquid to a boil again. Add the Madeira and enough stock for the sauce to fill the sauce dish. Once again, bring to a boil and then strain through a fine-mesh sieve.

Arrange the veal fillets in an oval or a circle on the serving platter. Place the carrots in the center and sprinkle with chopped parsley. Place a heaping teaspoon of mushroom duxelles on each fillet.

Serve with French beans, tied in bunches, and braised Belgian endives. ❧

3

Toward a
New Luxury

The Embers of a Vanishing World

On May 30, 1968, General de Gaulle drove up the Champs-Elysées to the cheers of thousands of Parisians. Among the enthusiastic crowd were men and women of all backgrounds, politicians, young people, students, executives, and employees, including chefs and cooks. After a month of general strikes and demonstrations, the President of the Republic had regained control of the situation. "*Les événements*" were over. Life could begin again, as carefree as ever. There was a sigh of relief all round.

At the same time, however, the Grenelle Agreements which brought the crisis to an end, had sanctioned a thirty-five percent increase in the minimum wage, a development that was to have far-reaching consequences, leading to the beginnings of inflation and social legislation that in a few years would see a considerable reduction in working hours. Wealth was shifting into new hands; lifestyles were undergoing a transformation.

But on that fine spring day, few paid any heed to all this. The strikes were over and the parties began anew. Alexis de Redé threw an oriental ball at the Hôtel Lambert at the tip of the Ile Saint-Louis. Guests were welcomed by Sikhs who held canopies aloft as they crossed the courtyard, where there stood a pair of white elephants decked in glittering caparisons. For the centenary of Proust's birth two years later, Guy and Marie-Hélène de Rothschild held her legendary Belle Epoque ball, attended by high society and Hollywood. These were the final flickers of a disappearing world. Alexis de Redé had received unambiguous signs of it in the form of letters of complaint from his neighbors, indignant about the disruption caused by his ball. Just fifteen years earlier, the inhabitants of Neuilly had crowded the pavements for all Arturo Lopez's parties, craning to catch a glimpse of the guests, eager to share a little of their glamor.

On the surface, life in society continued as before. Some forty chefs still manned the kitchens of the grand residences on the avenue Foch. But their days were numbered, and slowly but surely changes in society were eventually to lead to the complete transformation of their world.

PAGE 69 *The vault of the Hall of Mirrors*
at the Château de Versailles.
FACING PAGE *Oscar de la Renta and Alexis de Redé*
at the Oriental Ball in Paris, December 5, 1969.

71

Reducing Expenses

CHANGES IN FRANCE'S SOCIAL LEGISLATION MEANT THAT THE STATUS OF DOMESTIC EMPLOYEES WAS NOW brought into line with that of all other paid employees. While this represented great progress, it was also a double-edged sword for the grand traditions of Parisian entertaining. Gone were the days when people didn't count their hours and time off was a matter of mutual agreement. Now everything had to be accounted for, and the cost of employing domestic staff soared.

Employing a chef, a couple of commis chefs, a butler, a footman, a maid, and a chauffeur, plus extra staff for grand dinners, was now prohibitively expensive. Large private establishments were forced to reduce their staff, and gradually commis chefs and footmen disappeared, while butlers became an endangered species. Service and menus were both scaled down.

Yet, some of the great society hostesses continued. In the Duchess of Windsor's household, as in most of the grand houses of the upper echelons of society, unchanging rituals were set in stone. Dinner started with a consommé, followed by a fish course, a meat course, cheese, and dessert, sometimes accompanied by fruit. Each course was served from silver trays by a butler, with vegetables and accompaniments in separate dishes. Each table was waited upon by two butlers, who always offered second helpings—and as the serving of leftovers was out of the question, a fresh dish was prepared each time. In total, a dinner for twenty-four required three days' labor by four kitchen staff and six butlers.

GRILLED TURBOT WITH DIJON AND OLD-FASHIONED MUSTARD

GREEN ASPARAGUS AND BABY CARROTS

With the proportions I give here, you can serve this dish as an appetizer.
For a main dish, use larger fillets, which will need to be cooked slightly longer.

Serves 8

INGREDIENTS

1 shallot	1 heaping tablespoon whole grain old-fashioned mustard
1 medium carrot (3 oz./80 g)	1 teaspoon chopped tarragon
4 tablespoons (60 g) butter	8 turbot fillets, skin removed, about 5 oz. (150 g) apiece
1 heaping tablespoon Dijon mustard	A little oil for the fillets
2 cups (500 ml) fish fumet	Salt
24 baby carrots with their greens	Freshly ground pepper
24 green asparagus	1 small bunch curly parsley to garnish
¾ cup (200 ml) crème fraîche	

Peel and chop the shallot. Peel the carrot and dice it finely. In a small saucepan, melt the butter and lightly sauté the carrot, shallot, and Dijon mustard, stirring with a wooden spoon. Pour in the fish fumet and season with two grinds of pepper. Simmer until reduced to one-quarter.

Peel the baby carrots and trim their greens to about 1 inch (3 cm). Wash the asparagus and trim them to 2 ½ inches (6 cm) from the tip. Cook the vegetables separately in boiling salted water, simmering gently, until they are still slightly crunchy. Refresh them in cold water and place them in two separate dishes, covered with buttered parchment paper. Keep warm.

Stir the crème fraîche into the reduced sauce and, over low heat, process with an immersion blender until foamy. With a wooden spoon, stir in the whole grain old-fashioned mustard and chopped tarragon. Keep warm.

Preheat the oven to 400°F (200°C). Brush the turbot fillets lightly with oil and season with salt and pepper. Heat a skillet over high heat. Place the fillets in the skillet and grill them for no longer than 2 minutes on one side only. Arrange them in a large dish or baking sheet and finish cooking in the oven for 2 minutes.

To serve, arrange the turbot fillets on a serving platter in a fan shape with the narrower ends together. Opposite the wider ends, place, three by three, the carrots and the asparagus. Place small sprigs of parsley on the narrower ends of the fillets. Serve with the sauce in a sauce dish.

You may also brush the turbot fillets with mustard before cooking them. ᵃ

The Controversial Rise of Plated Service

WITH RISING PRICES AND SALARIES, IT WAS SIMPLY NOT POSSIBLE TO RETAIN THE FORMER LEVEL OF LUXURY, and savings were sought wherever they could be made. Instead of being served separately, vegetables were now arranged around the meat, so saving on one of the butlers. Plated service was inspired by Japanese traditions. It had the advantage of avoiding a second service, meaning that quantities could be calculated more accurately, but "good" families had always considered it rather beneath their dignity. Gaining its first toehold with meals organized by caterers, it gradually made its way up the social scale. Initially it was tolerated for the first course only, because of its practical advantages: placing the appetizer on the table before the guests arrived meant that the whole meal could be shorter. Then it penetrated some of the most stubbornly traditional households, still for the first course only, and occasionally for dessert. In the early years of the twenty-first century it made its appearance at the British Embassy, slipping in through the back door, though for working lunches only. Then it extended its reach to include some less formal dinners. After that it entered the portals of the Elysée Palace, for a rapid lunch or the occasional dinner, sometimes even for all three courses. The victory of plated service was complete.

At the same time, the number of courses started to shrink. From the 1970s the consommé course disappeared, and although the cheese course put up stiff resistance into the new millennium, it too eventually succumbed. Then it was no longer a fish course *and* a meat course, but rather a fish course *or* a meat course. Except at the grandest of occasions, there were now only three courses—an appetizer, a meat or fish course, and a dessert—a restaurant-style menu for the highest in the land!

Costing was now the norm, and chefs knuckled down. Whatever dish they were serving, from the most sophisticated timbale of lobster *à l'armoricaine* to the tiniest canapé, they had to work out the costs and write them all down—something that would have been unthinkable before. But, at the same time, there was no question of economizing on quality. The way to bring costs down was to make adjustments to the menu.

In James's view, the most expensive dishes are in any case not necessarily the best. Cuisine that is just as excellent but more reasonable in price can be created by selecting recipes that are less aristocratic but just as rich in flavor. A *farce*, for example, always used to be made with fillets of sole, pike, or pike-perch, which lent it great delicacy. Replacing these fish with whiting fillets spiced with a hint of *piment d'Espelette* produces a result that is different but equally delicious.

LAYERED ARTICHOKES AND FOIE GRAS

Serves 8

INGREDIENTS

1 lemon	2 tablespoons olive oil
8 globe artichokes	1 tablespoon white wine
1 tablespoon flour	Salt
1 lobe fresh duck foie gras	Freshly ground pepper
3 ½ tablespoons (50 g) butter, softened	8 tablespoons fig or pear chutney
Cayenne pepper	Lamb's lettuce or arugula (rocket) leaves
1 tablespoon Armagnac or cognac	1 sprig chervil to garnish

SPECIAL EQUIPMENT

Eight 2 ½-inch (6 cm) metal pastry rings or high ramekins of the same diameter.

Squeeze the lemon and pour the juice into a mixing bowl with 4 cups (1 l) water. Tear the stalk off the artichokes—this will pull off the lower fibers, which would stay if you simply cut the stalks. Cut the leaves right at the base but leave the choke. Peel the edge of the artichoke bottoms with a small knife and trim with a vegetable peeler, dropping them in the lemon water as you work so they do not discolor.

Stir the flour into a pot with 12 cups (3 l) boiling salted water. (The water into which a small quantity of flour is diluted is known as a *blanc*.) Bring the water back to a boil. Remove the artichoke bottoms from the lemon water and drain them. Drop them into the blanc and cook them for about 15 minutes, or until the choke can easily be pulled off. Drain them and remove the choke with a spoon. Let cool.

Remove the membrane from the foie gras and cut it into thin slices. Season with salt and pepper. Heat a pan and color the slices rapidly on both sides. Then push them through a sieve with the butter, or crush them with a fork. Stir in a knife tip's worth of Cayenne pepper and the Armagnac or cognac. Place in the refrigerator.

Line a baking sheet with parchment paper and place the rings on it; alternatively, line the bottom of the ramekins with parchment paper. Finely slice the artichoke bottoms and use these slices to cover the base of each ring. Spread the foie gras over the artichoke layer. Repeat the operation until you have four thin layers of artichokes and three slightly thicker layers of foie gras in each ring. Chill for at least 2 to 3 hours.

Twenty minutes before serving, slip the blade of a knife round the inside of the rings and turn out onto plates. Combine the oil and white wine to make a vinaigrette.

Just before serving, place a spoonful of chutney next to each layered round, and a few leaves of lamb's lettuce or arugula. Drizzle them with a little white wine vinaigrette. Sprinkle with freshly ground pepper and garnish with a chervil leaf.

If you are not fond of chutney, use peeled apple or pear quarters instead. I like to serve this dish with fine slices of toasted bread made with nuts and dried fruit. ❧

$\mathcal{I}$ngredients from around the World

LONG GONE ARE THE DAYS WHEN JAMES, AS A YOUNG APPRENTICE, USED TO "CANDLE" EGGS IN THE SPRING, when the hens laid most prolifically, so that they could be kept for up to a year. Any eggs that were cracked had to be discarded, so first of all they had to be held up (or candled) against a light bulb to have their shells checked. Then they were arranged in trays holding three thousand apiece, which were filled up with water and oatmeal. After a few days, a protective layer would form, which would enable them to go through the winter unscathed.

French cuisine of the past was based on seasonal fruits and vegetables from the kitchen garden. Winter was the time for vegetable purées and red and green cabbage, followed by vanilla, chocolate, or tutti-frutti ice cream for dessert. Apricot jellies and berry sorbets made their appearance in summer. Regional crops such as aubergines and even tomatoes were not generally available. English cooking, by contrast, made great use of spices, and over the years the two cuisines grew more alike. Alongside the traditional chives, parsley, and tarragon, French cuisine began to use new herbs and spices, such as fennel, cilantro, and many others. Vegetables are now imported from all over the world and are consumed throughout the year, regardless of whether or not they are in season. Root vegetables neglected since the end of the war, such as Jerusalem artichokes, swede, and parsnips, have returned to favor once more; and market stalls are stacked high with exotic fruits such as lychees, mangoes, and persimmons.

Some of the criteria for what constituted luxury ingredients are now turned on their heads. Salmon, for instance, has become an everyday item—with all the surprises that this can hold in store, as James recalls: "One day when I was cooking a wild salmon I smelt a powerful aroma of fuel oil. The fish must have swum alongside a ship out at sea. The 'wild' designation is not necessarily a guarantee of quality." Conversely, hake has now all but disappeared and cod, which used to be abundant and affordable, is now rarer and more expensive.

As far as poultry is concerned, real quality is now hard to find. "Only Bresse chicken is of true quality, and only if you buy it from a good supplier," James believes. Chicken flesh, being porous, tends to take on the flavor of the feed on which the birds have been fed. So if they are fed on fishmeal, for instance, the flesh tastes of fish. This led to intriguing (and swiftly abandoned) experiments in America, in which chickens were given feed designed to give their flesh an orange or lemon flavor.

SCOTTISH PRAWNS AND SPICY CRISP TRIANGLES

Serves 8

INGREDIENTS

28 medium prawns
Olive oil
Piment d'Espelette
16 green asparagus
1 ½ tablespoons (20 g) butter

2 sheets brik pastry (or phyllo)
Sesame and poppy seeds for sprinkling
2 Belgian endives, white or red
8 large arugula (rocket) leaves

For the verjuice sauce

1 large shallot
A few sprigs dill, leaves picked
Scant ½ cup (100 ml) crème fraîche
Scant ½ cup (100 ml) fish fumet
1 tablespoon wine vinegar
1 tablespoon verjuice
1 heaping teaspoon old-fashioned mustard with seeds
Sesame seeds

Poppy seeds
Piment d'Espelette
Salt
Freshly ground pepper
6 tablespoons curd cheese
8 sprigs chives, plus 1 teaspoon chopped chives
1 lemon

SPECIAL EQUIPMENT

One or two 3-inch (8 cm) diameter cardboard tubes covered with foil, which will fit in your oven.*

Separate the heads of the prawns from the tails and shell the tails. Place them in a dish, drizzle with olive oil, sprinkle with a little *piment d'Espelette*, and marinate while you continue working.

Trim the bases of the asparagus and either cook them for a few minutes in salted boiling water or steam them. They should retain some crunch, and the cooking time depends on their size.

Preheat the oven to 350°C (180°F). Melt 1 tablespoon (15 g) butter. Spread the sheets of brik over parchment paper and brush them with the butter. Sprinkle them with the sesame seeds, poppy seeds, and a little *piment d'Espelette*. Cut eight strips, each 1 x 6 ½ inches (2.5 x 16 cm). Then cut out eight isosceles triangles, with a base of 1 ¼ inches (3 cm) and 2 ¾-inch (7 cm) sides.

Place the foil-covered cardboard tube on a baking sheet. Drape the strips of pastry over the tube so that they form horseshoe shapes. Place the triangles on the baking sheet. Bake for 3 to 4 minutes, keeping a careful eye on them, until they are golden brown.

Heat a sauté pan. Cook the prawn tails for 2 minutes on each side and season them with salt. Remove from heat and let cool at room temperature.

SCOTTISH PRAWNS AND SPICY CRISP TRIANGLES (continued)

Make the sauce: Peel and chop the shallot. Snip the dill leaves. Combine the crème fraîche, fish fumet, vinegar, verjuice, shallot, dill, and mustard. Season with salt and pepper and add a pinch of *piment d'Espelette*. Add a few sesame and poppy seeds.

Combine the curd cheese with ½ to 1 tablespoon of the verjuice sauce and chopped chives. Keep 8 prawn tails whole. Cut the others in half lengthwise. Cut the lemon into 8 pieces lengthwise.

Arrange the plates on the work surface so that you can plate them simultaneously. To begin, place the prawn half-tails in the center, dotting some cheese between them. Place the horseshoe shaped pastry around it and stand the triangles against the opening of the horseshoe, keeping them in place with a whole prawn tail. Insert a chive sprig into the top. Place the small endive leaves on the plate and half-fill them with the remaining cheese. Add an arugula leaf, the asparagus spears, and a lemon quarter. Drizzle a circle of sauce around if you wish. ❧

* For this recipe, I keep a cardboard tube of the right dimensions and cover it each time with foil.

85

*T*hirty Seconds in the Blender *instead of Two Hours by Hand*

Another development was now also set to revolutionize cooking methods and dramatically cut preparation times: the advent of increasingly efficient food processors, blenders, and electric ice cream makers. "We used to do everything by hand," recalls James. "To make a *farce* we would pound the fish in a mortar, stir in a little cream with a spatula, and pass it all through a sieve of the appropriate mesh size: 25, 35, 42, or 45." There was a whole range of sieves, numbered according to the number of holes per square centimeter of mesh. Now, however, thirty seconds in the blender can replace two hours of preparation. Examples are too numerous to mention: for a *sauce armoricaine*, for example, gone are the days of mashing the ingredients, passing them through a fine sieve and finally pressing them through muslin in order to obtain a velvety smooth velouté. Now a food processor does it all. And for a *sauce verte* there is no need now to poach the green leaves—parsley, spinach, and watercress—before filtering them through muslin to collect the chlorophyll, then mixing it into the mayonnaise. You just put all the leaves in a blender. This is progress that no cook could have dreamed of a few decades ago.

While he appreciates that such time-saving gadgets place proper cooking within the reach of many less experienced cooks, James also confesses to a touch of nostalgia for the old ways: "We lived with the raw ingredients, we worked them with our hands. When you chop parsley by hand, you can chop it precisely as fine as you need it. When you knead brioche dough, you can gauge how elastic it is and add eggs or flour accordingly."

87

CROWN OF FISH ARMORICAINE

Serves 8

INGREDIENTS

1 lobster weighing 1 ¼ lb. (600 g)	Scant ½ cup (100 ml) Calvados or other apple brandy
2 large shallots	3 ½ cups (900 ml) dry white wine, divided
8 oz. (250 g) ripe tomatoes	Cayenne pepper
1 ¾ sticks (200 g) butter, divided	Salt
2 tablespoons olive oil, divided	Freshly ground pepper

For the crown

1 lb. 2 oz. (500 g) white fish fillets	1 ½ cups (350 ml) heavy cream
2 egg whites	

For the garnish

16 small potatoes, shaped like olives	3 peppercorns, crushed
1 tablespoon flour	16 Portobello mushrooms, white or brown
4 ½ lb. (2 kg) mussels	14 oz. (400 g) small button mushrooms
2 sprigs thyme	1 slice lemon
½ bay leaf	1 tablespoon crème fraîche
1 sprig parsley	1 bunch chives

For the court-bouillon

1 small carrot	1 small sprig thyme
5 peppercorns	1 sprig parsley
½ bay leaf	Salt

For the sauce, first make the court-bouillon: Peel the carrot and slice it finely. Crush the peppercorns. Pour 8 cups (2 l) water into a pot and add the bay leaf, thyme, parsley, carrot, peppercorns, and salt. Bring to a boil and simmer for 30 minutes.

Drop the lobster into the court-bouillon. Bring to a boil again and let simmer gently for 20 minutes. Remove the lobster from the pot. Separate the tail from the body, extract the flesh, and slice it finely. Remove the flesh from the claws and cut it into small dice. Cut the head into two and discard the small grey pouch of gravel. With a large knife, crush the claws and the contents of the head on a board.

Peel and chop 1 shallot. Peel the tomatoes, remove the seeds, and chop them roughly. Melt 3 ½ tablespoons (50 g) butter with 1 tablespoon olive oil in a sauté pan. Cook the chopped lobster head and claws with the chopped shallot until lightly colored. Pour in the Calvados and flambé it. Add the chopped tomatoes, 2 cups (500 ml) white wine, and a pinch of Cayenne pepper. Season with salt and pepper. Cover with the lid and cook over low heat for no more than 20 minutes, otherwise the sauce will taste too strongly of the shell. Strain the sauce through a fine-mesh sieve and reduce until you have the quantity needed to fill a sauce dish.

For the crown: Preheat the oven to 350°F (180°C). In a food processor, process the fish fillet and egg whites using the blade knife until the mixture is very finely chopped. Push through a fine-mesh sieve into a mixing bowl placed over ice. Gradually add the heavy cream, stirring it in with a flexible spatula. Season with salt and pepper and add a pinch of Cayenne pepper.

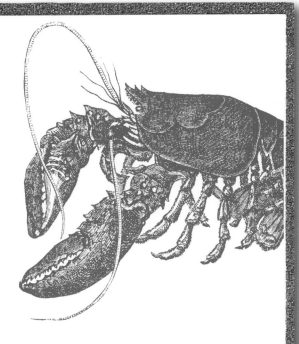

Grease a turban-shaped mold generously with butter. Pour in the fish preparation and place the mold into a dish filled with very hot water. Bake for 30 minutes. After 15 minutes, cover the crown with a sheet of buttered parchment paper. Make sure that the water does not boil while the fish crown is cooking.

For the garnish: Clean and wash the potatoes and steam them. Keep warm.

Make a white roux: Melt 4 tablespoons (60 g) butter in a small sauté pan. When it is sizzling, add 1 heaping tablespoon flour and stir constantly with a wooden spoon for 1 minute. Do not allow the roux to color. Remove from heat and let cool.

Scrape the mussels and wash them. Peel and chop 1 shallot. Place the mussels in a large pot with the ¾ cup (200 ml) wine (keep in mind that the mussels will render a lot of liquid), shallot, 4 tablespoons (60 g) butter, thyme, ½ bay leaf, sprig of parsley, and the crushed peppercorns. Do not add any salt as the mussels exude salty water. Cover with the lid and cook over high heat, keeping an eye on them. They must not cook for too long, as they will become rubbery. As soon as they open, remove them from heat, drain, and take them out of their shells. Return them to the cooking liquid.

Clean the Portobello mushrooms by wiping them. Decorate them by drawing a flower shape with the tip of a knife or use a canelle (grooving knife). Place them in a saucepan with the remaining ¾ cup (200 ml) white wine, 1 slice lemon, 1 sprig thyme, ½ bay leaf, 1 tablespoon olive oil, salt, and pepper. Cover with the lid and cook over high heat for 4 minutes. Remove the mushrooms with a slotted spoon (you will need the cooking liquid for the next step) and keep them warm in a bowl, covered with buttered parchment paper. Clean the smaller mushrooms and cook them in the same liquid for 2 minutes. Remove them with a slotted spoon and keep warm.

Strain the mussel cooking liquid and the mushroom cooking liquid into a saucepan. Heat them together. With a small whisk, gradually incorporate the roux. Cook gently until the sauce is the desired consistency. Remove from heat and add the mussels, button mushrooms, diced lobster claws, and crème fraîche. Keep warm, but do not let boil.

Melt 1 ½ tablespoons (20 g) butter and pour it over the potatoes. Scatter them with snipped chives. Turn out the crown onto a serving platter. Around it, alternate the Portobello mushrooms and potatoes. With a slotted spoon, transfer the mixture of mussels and button mushrooms to make a pyramid in the center of the crown. Place the slices of lobster tail around the base of the pyramid inside the crown. Stud 3 sprigs of chives into the mussels. Serve the sauce in a separate bowl. Add small leaves of other herbs if you wish.

Sometimes, instead of serving bread with this dish, I make small savory scones with chives or chopped onion lightly fried in butter. ❧

Cooking made Easy

THESE DAYS WE NEVER HAVE ENOUGH TIME OR ENOUGH MONEY, AND COOKING HAS GRADUALLY BECOME simpler to reflect this. Yet never has it been so fêted and celebrated. Once it would have been unthinkable to discuss recipes at table. Excellence was taken for granted, and congratulating the hostess on a delicious dish was tantamount to committing a social gaffe. Today, by contrast, we discuss recipes, make a note of ingredients, and generally savor and enjoy the dishes we are served.

Behind this transformation in attitudes, according to James, are two of his fellow chefs: Paul Bocuse and Raymond Olivier. Paul Bocuse brought the profession to public attention when he was decorated with the Légion d'honneur by the French President. And Raymond Olivier introduced cooking to French television screens, so beaming it directly into French homes.

No chef working in a private household had ever before appeared on French television when the first cookery program was broadcast in a series fronted by Olivier and the popular presenter Catherine Langeais. When the idea was suggested to him, the chef grasped immediately how beneficial the series could be for his restaurant. He threw himself into the idea, and the series was soon gaining large audiences and encouraging a new enthusiasm for cooking that has never since ceased to grow.

Virtually overnight, chefs became celebrities and cordon bleu cooking became a career to which one could aspire to. Sometimes there were disappointments. Youngsters clamored for places at catering schools, but were often discouraged when they discovered the harsh realities of the job. Nonetheless, at the very point when financial constraints and the changing face of Paris society meant that private domestic chefs were a vanishing species, chefs working in restaurants and grand hotels were becoming media stars.

These chefs have a different job to do. Restaurant chefs offer their clientele a handful of their particular specialties, which form the foundation of their reputation. Their repertoire is therefore more restricted, but they also have important administrative and business responsibilities. It is they who must shoulder the financial risks of an empty dining room. Once, in 1965, James was tempted to buy a restaurant in Chantilly. Before his wife pulled him back from the brink.

Chefs in Paris' grand hotels, by contrast, have fewer administrative responsibilities, and are concerned only with gastronomic matters. In the 1970s, the Hôtel Crillon became the first to put a team of fifty or sixty kitchen staff and an unlimited budget at the disposal of its greatest chefs. The city's other grand hotels, the Plaza, the Meurice, and the Bristol, followed suit, vying with each other in the unfettered pursuit of excellence. While their income depended on other factors, their reputation rested on their cuisine.

GRILLED RED MULLET

Serves 8

INGREDIENTS

8 red mullet, fins removed, scaled, and gutted
4 large fennel bulbs
16 cocktail tomatoes
7 oz. (200 g) porcini
7 oz. (200 g) chanterelles
7 oz. (200 g) morels
1 large shallot
1 ½ tablespoons olive oil

Juice of 1 large lemon
Ground fennel seeds
2 tablespoons (30 g) butter
Flour for dusting
Salt
Freshly ground pepper
A few sprigs of parsley or fennel to garnish
Lemon quarters or melted butter with
    a little lemon juice to serve

For the marinade: Combine the lemon juice, olive oil, ground fennel seeds, salt, and pepper. Make three incisions on both sides of each mullet. Place them side by side in a rectangular dish and pour over the marinade. Chill for at least 1 hour, turning them over from time to time.

Clean the fennel and cut off the small green leaves. Set them aside. Place the fennel bulbs in a large pot of boiling salted water and cook for about 20 minutes. They should remain slightly firm—test with the tip of a knife, which should slide in easily.

Cut off the tops of the tomatoes, reserving the caps. Hollow out the tomatoes with a teaspoon. Season the insides with salt and place them upside down on paper towel so that the liquid drains out.

Clean the porcini with paper towel or a damp cloth. Cut off the bottom of the stalks of the chanterelles and wash them rapidly without allowing them to soak. Press them gently in a cloth to remove any excess water. Cut off the bottom of the stalks of the morels and wash them carefully to remove any earth and gravel. Press them gently in a cloth to dry.

Cut the three types of mushroom separately into small pieces.

Peel and chop the shallot. Heat ½ tablespoon oil in a pan over high heat and sauté one third of the chopped shallot with the porcini for a few minutes. Remove them. Add ½ tablespoon oil and another third of the shallot to the pan and sauté the chanterelles. Repeat with the morels. Mix the three types together and fill the tomatoes with the mixture. Top with the cap and keep warm.

Drain the fennel and cut into quarters lengthwise. Dust in a little flour and brown briefly in a sauté pan with the butter. Keep warm.

Heat a skillet until very hot. Drain the mullet and place them on the skillet. Cook for 2 minutes on each side. Keep warm.

Place the mullet in a fan shape on a serving platter so that the tails touch. Between the heads, place 2 tomatoes and 4 fennel quarters shaped to make a whole bulb. Garnish the tails with a sprig of parsley or a few fennel leaves.

Serve with lemon quarters or melted butter to which you can add lemon juice and fennel leaves. ❧

4 THE GREAT TRADITION TODAY

$\mathscr{N}$ew Social Codes for "Le Tout-Paris"

"It all came to an end thirty years ago." Philippine de Rothschild is categorical: entertaining is still important, but receptions and parties do not have the same *raison d'être*. The tone is no longer set by prominent society figures who entertain purely for pleasure. Grand occasions have become a publicity tool, the preserve of high-end companies anxious to polish their image. After filtering down from the aristocracy to the wealthy bourgeoisie and intellectuals who formed what was known as "le Tout-Paris," entertaining is now open to everyone, and perhaps especially to those who have found success in the media spotlight.

PAGES 100–101 *The Tapestry Dining Room*
at the British Ambassador's Residence in Paris.
These Brussels tapestries depict rustic pursuits,
after cartoons by David Teniers II and III.
They abound in charming details.

$\mathcal{E}$mbassies: The Last Refuge

Chefs have thus found refuge with a fortunate few who include the David-Weills, David and Benjamin de Rothschild, Edouard de Ribes, and Isabelle d'Ornano. Catherine Aga Khan, widow of Sadruddin Aga Khan, still employs two. But it is in Paris' embassies, in the Elysée Palace, and in the private dining rooms of some banks that the great chefs continue to practice their skills.

When James Viaene went to work at the British Embassy in 1970, he could scarcely have imagined that he would still be there forty years later. It was here that he was able to give full rein to all he had learned in the grand households in which he had worked, and to allow his skills to truly blossom. As Lady Westmacott, wife of Sir Peter Westmacott, (ambassador from 2007 to 2012) points out with a smile, in France the principal preoccupation after politics is the table. Guests expect excellence, and they appreciate it. The kitchen is therefore the heart of the Embassy, and the chef a figure of central importance.

In keeping with the changing times, protocol in this imposing *hôtel particulier* in the Faubourg-Saint-Honoré—once home to Napoleon's sister, Pauline Borghese—has become more relaxed over the last four decades. Meals are shorter now. Lunches are much shorter, with coffee sometimes served at the table rather than in the drawing room; dinner goes on a little longer but certainly not forever, drawing to a close by eleven o'clock, or eleven thirty at the latest.

Receptions may be slightly less formal, but they are still a constant feature of embassy life. Whether it be for a lunch for forty guests, a dinner for eighty, or cocktails for one hundred and twenty, some sixteen thousand guests are invited to the Ambassador's Residence every year. Unforeseen events and last-minute changes of plan are a fact of life. British ministers stay at the residence when they are visiting Paris, and their timetables are fluid. They may emerge from a meeting at the Elysée Palace, a stone's throw away, feeling ravenous, or they may decide to dine at home after going to the theater instead of going on to a restaurant as arranged. On one occasion, a lunch for twenty Members of Parliament metamorphosed the night before into a reception for two hundred and fifty guests. Whatever the challenge, James never failed to rise to it.

The division of labor within the Embassy staff is laid down according to an unchanging ritual. Everyone has his or her role. The butler oversees the serving staff and acts as sommelier, selecting wines and presenting them to the ambassador who makes his selection. Great French vintages are highly prized, but often the butler will choose wines that are genuine "finds," of great quality but at affordable prices. The kitchen is the chef's domain. As well as devising menus and proposing them to the ambassador's wife, who discusses them with him and approves them, he also supervises the commis chefs and is in charge of ordering supplies.

FACING PAGE *The British Ambassador's Residence in Paris seen from the garden.*

Lancashire Hotpot

MEDIEVAL
ENGLISH FARE

Lancashire hotpot never features on the menu for official Embassy dinners, nor does the ambassador serve it to his British guests. Instead it is reserved exclusively for French guests who are interested in discovering authentic English specialties. This is the dish that embodies popular English cooking perhaps more than any other. Medieval in origin and still a British Army staple and pub food perennial, it has been a favorite of several ambassadors' wives, who have passed on their recipes to James. This slow-cooked stew of lamb, onions, and carrots, flavored with thyme and bay leaf, moistened with stock and traditionally topped with sliced potatoes, is both easy and relatively inexpensive to make. For a more elegant variation, James suggests serving it in tartlets filled with the various ingredients and topped with a marguerite of lamb: traditional country style meets contemporary chic.

LANCASHIRE HOTPOT

LAMB DAISIES

I have made several versions of this dish. Here is one that I served as tartlets at the Embassy.

Serves 6

INGREDIENTS

1 large carrot (3 ½ oz./100 g)
1 medium floury potato (3 ½ oz./100 g)
1 shallot (¾ oz./20 g)
1 leek, white part only (3 ½ oz./100 g)
10 oz. (300 g) shoulder of lamb
4 ½ tablespoons (70 g) butter
1 cup (250 ml) lamb stock, made with
   the bones of the rack
1 small sprig thyme

1 bay leaf
2 small racks of lamb, fat and bones removed
2 hard-boiled eggs
6 3-inch tartlet shells (8 cm), puff pastry or short pastry
1 tablespoon chopped parsley
Salt
Freshly ground pepper

Peel the carrot, potato, and shallot. Wash the leek and cut it in half lengthwise. Cut all the vegetables into fine dice. Finely dice the shoulder of lamb.

In a large, heavy pot, melt the butter and gently brown the fillets from the racks of lamb for 4 minutes, until they are well colored all over. Transfer them to a plate and cover them with parchment paper to let them continue to cook.

Place all the diced vegetables and diced lamb shoulder in the same pot with the potato (which will thicken the cooking juices). Season lightly with salt and add the pepper. Add the lamb stock, thyme, and bay leaf. Bring to a boil, cover with the lid, and let simmer over low heat for 20 minutes. Remove the pot from heat and let rest in a warm place for 20 minutes.

Cut the lamb fillets into ¼-inch (5 mm) slices. Shell the hard-boiled eggs and scoop out the yolks; you will not need the whites. Mash the yolks and shape them into six small balls.

To serve, slightly warm the tartlet shells. Place one on each plate. Using a spoon, divide the diced vegetable and lamb mixture evenly among the tartlet shells and sprinkle with chopped parsley. Arrange the slices of lamb on top of the vegetables to form the petals of the daisy. Place a small ball of egg yolk in the middle to form the yellow center of the daisy. Drizzle a little sauce on the side.

Serve the tartlets with peas, chopped broccoli, or small steamed potatoes coated with butter and sprinkled with freshly chopped mint.

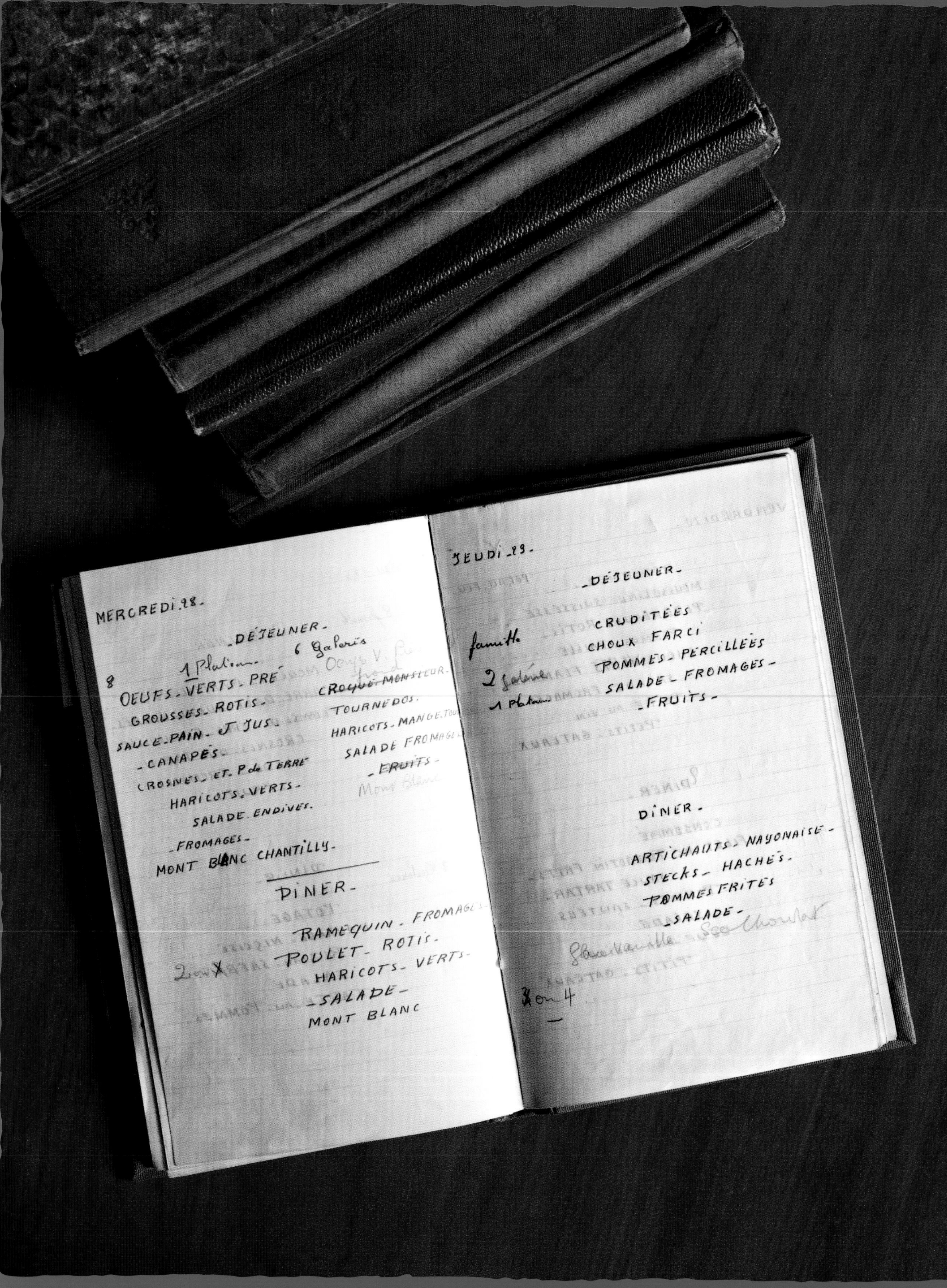

MERCREDI. 28.

-DÉJEUNER-
8   1 Plateau   6 Galeris
OEUFS. VERTS. PRÉ   Oeufs V. Pré
                            froid
GROUSSES. ROTIS.   CROQUE MONSIEUR.
SAUCE. PAIN. J. JUS.   TOURNEDOS.
 - CANAPÉS.   HARICOTS. MANGE. TOUT
CROSNES. ET. P. de TERRE   SALADE FROMAGE.
HARICOTS. VERTS.   - FRUITS -
SALADE. ENDIVES.   Mont Blanc
- FROMAGES -
MONT BLANC CHANTILLY.

        DINER -
        RAMEQUIN. FROMAGE.
2 ou X   POULET. ROTIS.
         HARICOTS. VERTS.
         SALADE -
         MONT BLANC

JEUDi. 29.
        -DÉJEUNER-
famille   CRUDITÉES
         CHOUX FARCI
2 galeris POMMES. PERCILLÉES
1 Plateau SALADE - FROMAGES -
              - FRUITS -

         - DINER -
         ARTICHAUTS. MAYONAISE -
         STECKS - HACHÉS -
         POMMES FRITES
         SALADE -
         Glace Vanille   Chocolat
3 ou 4 -

As a variation, I add a scoop of a country-style purée like Scottish champ or Irish colcannon. Traditionally, cooking liquid and buttermilk were added to these purées to soften them; I prefer milk and cream. In addition to these purées, you can add a small tomato filled with softened red onion.

These delicious country purées are very easy to make:

For Irish colcannon, roughly mash 2 ½ lb. (1 kg) cooked potatoes with a fork. Chop 1 large yellow or white onion and sauté it with 2 tablespoons (30 g) butter. Shred 2 green cabbage leaves, boil them for 3 minutes and drain them. Add the onion and cabbage to the mashed potatoes. Then add 1 tablespoon chopped chives, 7 tablespoons (100 g) butter, and enough heavy cream to bring the purée to the desired consistency. Season with salt and pepper.

To make Scottish champ, roughly mash 2 ½ lb. (1 kg) cooked potatoes with a fork. Finely slice a leek and soften it well in butter. Combine it with the mashed potatoes and add 1 tablespoon chopped chives. Stir in butter and cream until the potatoes reach the desired consistency and season with salt and pepper. I also use spring onions or shredded arugula (rocket).

For the Scottish purée known as rumbledethumps, combine mashed potato, green cabbage, and onion in a gratin dish. Sprinkle with cheddar and bake. It is also very good with Stilton. ☙

FACING PAGE *Some of James Viaene's lovingly preserved notebooks containing his menu suggestions.*
PAGE 111 *The Salon Rouge at the British Ambassador's Residence is occasionally used for intimate dinners— portrait of the Duke of Wellington (1769–1852) and Lord Stuart de Rothesay (1779–1845), former British ambassadors, contemplate the richly laid table.*

$\mathcal{G}$ourmet Ambassadors

WHILE THE CHEF PROPOSES MENUS, THE TONE IS SET BY THE AMBASSADOR. JAMES HAS KNOWN TEN, MOST of them highly discerning connoisseurs of food and wine. First came Sir Christopher Soames, Churchill's son-in-law, who maintained that chefs were not bold enough in their choices, and asked James for country dishes such as cassoulet, *boeuf bourguignonne*, calves' liver, and offal, more interesting than the classic fillet of beef. He would also test him by laying traps for him: "Make me *aiguillettes de boeuf* for tomorrow night," he might ask, knowing full well that it was impossible to make this dish in such a short time. "I'll make it, but you'll be disappointed," the equally diplomatic James would reply. Like Soames, Sir Ewen Fergusson, another gourmet, was also fond of some nineteenth-century dishes that were disappearing, such as *chartreuses de faisan* and *Pompadour de canard*, a sort of sophisticated terrine based on a *farce* of duck, truffles, and veal sweetbreads. He was also a fine connoisseur of wine. One evening he joined the staff in the kitchen for a wine tasting. He eliminated the least distinguished contender by nose alone, before going on to a virtually faultless blind tasting of the remaining vintages, an impressive feat that earned him the respect of the entire team. For Lady Fretwell, who had a penchant for desserts that were as seductive to the eye as they were to the palate, James created veritable works of art in "*pastillage*," made from icing sugar, egg white, and a little gelatin. Among his masterpieces were a Spitfire for a World War II pilot, and, for a British artist, a romantic confection consisting of plinths in icing topped by the almond-paste figure of a marquise gazing at a chocolate painting displayed on a nougatine easel.

Lady Westmacott, for her part, loved the chef's *tours de force*, such as stuffed turbot, beef Wellington, honey-roasted duck, that are the epitome of haute cuisine, while Lady Henderson was so impressed by James's recipes that she published them in book form.

Should the British Embassy serve British cuisine, to promote the United Kingdom, or French cuisine? Lady Holmes opted for resolutely British fare, imposing a complete embargo on *sauce mousseline*, a controversy into which James refused to be drawn. Tastes change, and in London habits have changed with them. Now, great chefs from around the world are lauded and fêted, especially in the upper echelons of society. The two cuisines have moved closer to each other, and the chef at the British Embassy is now able to create menus that are wholly French, while adding a few British touches. Bacon and eggs are now served for breakfast only when there are guests. But other specialties also add a dash of cross-Channel charm, such as Welsh lamb, kidney beans cooked with brown sugar (a delicious and neglected form of home-made baked beans), and kedgeree, the creamy risotto with hard-boiled eggs, smoked haddock, and a curry sauce that arrived from imperial India to conquer Victorian and Edwardian breakfast buffets. But James steers well clear of the garish and very solid fruit jellies that are a staple of children's parties across the Channel. The one and only occasion on which he tackled them, for a children's tea, he used fresh fruit, a flavor so far removed from the children's expectations that they left them on their plates, untouched. Thereafter, James bought the ready-made variety from Marks & Spencer!

$\mathcal{T}$he Banqueting Table

They are a vanishing species. The last State Dinner was as long ago as 2006. Even for great occasions, ambassadors today prefer a less formal and more convivial style of entertaining. And it has to be said that the banqueting table is so vast in its proportions (measuring two and a half meters across) that it is completely impossible for guests facing each other across it to keep up any kind of conversation at all. But there is no more gorgeous or splendid a sight, all the same, than the banqueting table in all its finery. Setting the table— a two-and-half-day epic involving four people—is an art in itself. To start with, twenty-eight extra leaves have to be put in place and covered with thick felting. The tablecloth—all seventeen meters of it—is then spread, before being ironed in situ for two hours until the tiniest crease is banished. Then the Empire ormolu trays are put in position as the table centerpiece and the flowers are arranged. The dinner service is fine, though not exceptional, as the same Minton service is used in every British embassy throughout the world.

Fifty-eight is the ideal number of guests to have around the great banqueting table, waited upon by a carefully choreographed phalanx of waiters beneath the immense crystal chandeliers. A great art indeed, now presented once a year to an eager public that waits in line several hours to see it on Paris' Patrimony Day.

FACING PAGE AND PAGES 114–115 *The State Dining Room at the British Ambassador's Residence in Paris. The dining table can accomodate fifty-eight people, and is laid with the magnificent Empire centerpiece by Thomire which has been at the Embassy since the early nineteenth century. The table is set as for the State Dinner on Patrimony Day, the day when the public can visit government buildings and embassies throughout France.*

*R*egal Delights

She is discreet and attentive, and she likes her meals—especially the meat course—lightly seasoned and served in small portions. This is what James recalls from cooking for Queen Elizabeth II on three occasions.
On the first occasion, in 1957, he was a commis chef at the Elysée Palace, and President de Gaulle was entertaining Elizabeth II on a state visit to Paris. Still very young, and barely out of his apprenticeship with the Duchess of Windsor, on this occasion he did no more than decorate the mousses de foie gras—*an honor that he would never forget, however.*
When the Queen returned to France fifteen years later, in May 1972, to mark Britain's entry into the European Union, James was the chef at the British Embassy, where she stayed for three days. Her days began with an early morning cup of tea, which she thoughtfully insisted on making herself in order not to put anyone else out. The menus were drawn up in consultation with the Elysée, taking care to ensure that every meal featured different dishes. The presidential palace opted for lobster timbales and lamb, while the Embassy chose salmon and fillet of beef. Forewarned of the royal tastes, James "cut down" the roasts, serving smaller slices and using the offcuts to make a beef Stroganoff. Before she left, the Queen awarded the chef the prestigious Royal Victorian Medal.

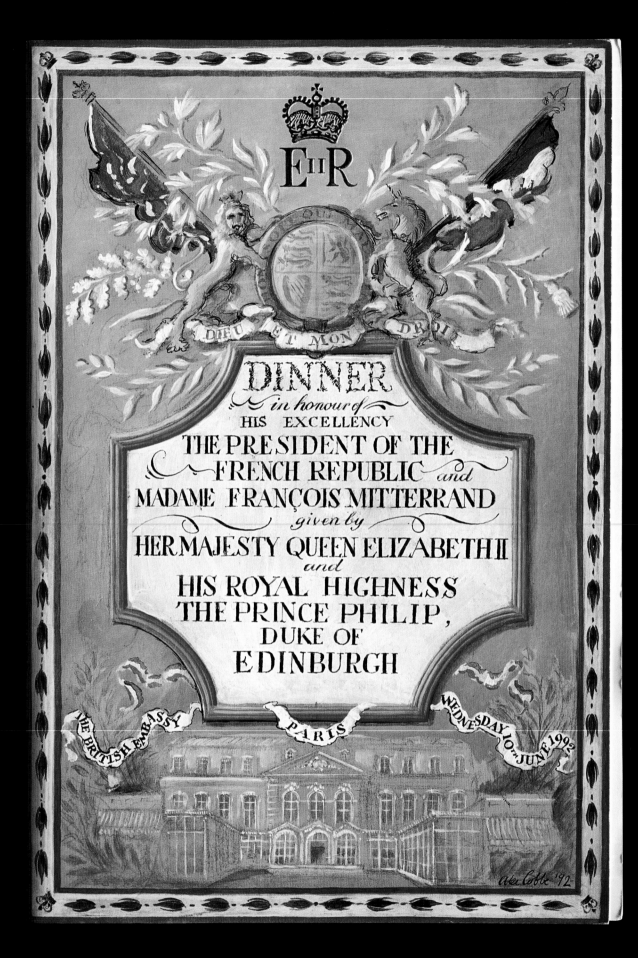

*Then she attended a reception at which the Embassy staff
were presented to her. Protocol was strict: ladies were not to wear
pant suits, the Queen was to be addressed as "Madame"
and the Duke of Edinburgh as "Monseigneur," and a respectful
distance was to be kept by all. At the same time, these meticulous
instructions displayed a considerable degree of thought
toward the staff. The Queen did not wish anyone to go to any
unnecessary expense: whatever normal protocol might say,
if the ladies did not possess a hat or gloves, there was really
no need to rush out and buy them.
In November 1998, the Queen paid a third visit to Paris, this time
in order to inaugurate a statue of Winston Churchill, accompanied
by Churchill's daughter, Lady Soames. For this occasion,
James prepared more British dishes, including her favorite
beef Wellington and* glace à la marmelade.
*James Viaene was a long way from his pots and pans
when he met the Queen another time. In the spring of 1996,
at a reception given at Buckingham Palace in honor of holders
of the Royal Victorian Medal, the Queen recognized the chef
and offered him her congratulations: a tribute that
he never fails to recall with emotion.*

FACING PAGE *Album made for a dinner hosted
by the Queen at the British Embassy in Paris in 1992,
in honor of François and Danielle Mitterrand.*

HEREFORD BEEF WELLINGTON

There are several ways of preparing this beef fillet. Here is mine,
which I always served with great success at the Embassy.
I like to use Hereford beef: the quality is excellent and the fillet is not too large,
which makes it easy to work with.

Serves 8

INGREDIENTS

3 tablespoons oil, divided	1 small truffle
5 tablespoons (75 g) butter, divided	3 lb. (1.3 kg) puff pastry
3 ¼ lb. (1.5 kg) beef fillet	1 egg yolk
1 large shallot	1 tablespoon milk
1 lb. 2 oz. (500 g) button mushrooms, white or cremini	Salt
1 tablespoon tomato paste	Freshly ground pepper
7 oz. (200 g) raw foie gras	

For the garnish

8 Belgian endives	2 ¼ lb. (1 kg) green beans
Juice of ½ lemon	3 long carrots
1 small onion	1 bunch watercress and
3 ½ tablespoons (50 g) butter, divided	Madeira sauce to serve
3 ¼ lb. (1.5 kg) pumpkin	

Heat 2 tablespoons oil and 1 ½ tablespoons (20 g) butter over high heat in a large pan. Brown the beef fillet on all sides and let cool.

Peel the shallot and chop it very finely. Trim the sandy base of the mushroom stems. Wash the mushrooms and cut them into small cubes. Press them in a clean cloth to remove any excess water. Heat 1 tablespoon oil and 2 tablespoons (30 g) butter in a sauté pan. Add the shallot and mushrooms. When they begin to brown, add the tomato paste and season with salt and pepper. Let simmer for a few minutes and transfer to a mixing bowl. Cover with a plate.

Remove the membrane from the foie gras and cut it into very thin slices, under ⅛ inch (3 mm) thick. Remove any visible veins and dip the slices into the flour. Melt 1 ½ tablespoons (20 g) butter in a large sauté pan and color the foie gras for a few minutes. Cut it into small dice and combine with the mushrooms. Finely chop the truffle and add it to the mixture. Let it cool, otherwise it will melt the butter in the puff pastry when spread over it.

Take 2 ¼ lb. (1 kg) of the puff pastry and roll it into a rectangle. It should be very thin, less than ⅛ inch (3 mm). Spread the mushroom and foie gras mixture evenly over the pastry, leaving a border of 1 ½ inches (4 cm) around the edge. Brush the edge lightly with water. Place the beef fillet in the center over the mushrooms and fold the puff pastry over it. Make sure the edges of the pastry are well stuck together. Turn it over onto a baking sheet. Dilute the egg yolk with the milk and brush the pastry.

Roll out the remaining puff pastry and with a pastry cutter, cut out small strips or leaf shapes. Place them over the fillet, criss-crossing them to form a lattice. Brush them with the egg yolk and milk mixture. Let rest for 15 minutes.

Preheat the oven to 400°F (200°C).

Cook the beef in the pastry for 30 to 40 minutes, depending on how thick the fillet is. Keep an eye on it as it cooks: if the pastry seems to be browning too quickly, cover it with parchment paper. The pastry should be golden. Let the cooked meat rest for 15 to 20 minutes.

Prepare the garnish: Remove the outer leaves of the Belgian endives and cook for 20 minutes over low heat in boiling salted water with lemon juice. Drain, reserving the liquid, and cut in half lengthwise. Fold each half over on itself. Generously butter a sauté pan and place the Belgian endive halves around the pan. Pour in enough cooking liquid to half cover them. Cover with a round of parchment paper and cook until all the liquid has evaporated. The bottom of the vegetables should be well colored.

Meanwhile, peel and chop the onion. Brown it well with 1 ½ tablespoons (20 g) butter.

Peel the pumpkin and cut the flesh into small dice. Blanch in boiling water for 2 minutes and drain. Combine with the onion and sauté in a pan with 2 tablespoons (30 g) butter until tender.

Trim and wash the beans, then cook, uncovered, in boiling salted water, making sure they retain their crunch.

Peel the carrots and cut into long ribbons. Cook for a few minutes in boiling water; they should remain fairly crunchy.

Drain the beans and carrots. Tie the beans into bunches with a carrot ribbon. Trim the edges so that they are all the same length.

Keep the vegetables warm.

Carefully cut the fillet of beef with a very sharp knife or a knife with a serrated edge. Place the slices on a serving platter, surrounded by alternating vegetables. Decorate with a bunch of watercress. Serve with Madeira sauce.

For a less costly version of this dish, I use chicken livers soaked in milk and sautéed like the foie gras. You can also replace the truffle with truffle-flavored oil.

For the Madeira sauce, a base known as "Espagnole" sauce was used in the past. It would take an entire day to prepare. Here is a simpler version: Cut the trimmings of the fillet into small pieces. Cut a small onion and small carrot into pieces. Color them well in a small saucepan. Add a heaping teaspoon of tomato paste and 2 cups (500 ml) water brought to a boil in the pot in which the meat was browned. Let the sauce cook for 40 minutes.

Strain through a fine-meshed sieve. Dilute ½ teaspoon cornstarch with 2 tablespoons Madeira and add it to the sauce. Bring to a boil, stirring constantly, until it thickens. Madeira wine should not boil too much or it becomes bitter. ❧

123

MARMALADE ICE CREAM

Serves 8

INGREDIENTS

½ vanilla bean, slit in half lengthwise
3 cups (750 ml) whole milk
8 egg yolks
¾ cup (5 oz./150 g) sugar
1 heaping tablespoon crème fraîche

⅔ cup (7 oz./200 g) orange marmalade
7 oz. (200 g) bittersweet baking chocolate
7 oz. (200 g) candied orange peel
1 small genoise sponge
Whipped cream or orange quarters to garnish

Place the slit vanilla bean it in a saucepan with the milk and heat. While it is coming to a boil, in a mixing bowl or a food processor, whisk the egg yolks with the sugar until the mixture is pale and thick.

Gradually pour the boiling milk over the egg and sugar mixture, whisking constantly. Return the liquid to the saucepan and heat, stirring constantly, until it is on the point of boiling and coats the back of a spoon. Remove from heat immediately (it must not boil). Let cool completely, stirring from time to time. Stir the crème fraîche into the custard mixture. Strain through a fine-mesh sieve. Place in an ice cream maker and follow the instructions. If you do not have an ice cream maker, freeze the mixture, stirring from time to time, until it reaches the consistency of ice cream.

When the ice cream has set, stir in the orange marmalade. Place the ice cream in a mold, preferably dome shaped (a small disposable plastic 4-cup or 1 liter container will do, as it is easy to unmold). Freeze until hardened, 2 to 3 hours.

Break the chocolate into pieces and melt gently over a bain-marie or in short pulses in the microwave, taking care not to scorch it. The temperature of the chocolate must not exceed 98°F (37°C), or normal body temperature, otherwise it will whiten as it cools. Skewer the pieces of candied orange peel individually on toothpicks and dip each one into the melted chocolate. Place the toothpicks on a base (a large colander turned upside down, for example). Let the chocolate harden, then remove the toothpicks from the coated peel, and chill.

Cut the sponge in half horizontally. Place one half on the serving dish. Dip the bottom of the mold into hot water for 3 seconds and turn the ice cream out onto the sponge. If you have used a plastic container, a hole pierced into the bottom will enable the ice cream to come out easily.

Insert the chocolate-coated orange peel into the ice cream so that it looks like a hedgehog. Garnish the base with whipped cream or orange quarters.

You can vary the richness of the ice cream. Proportions range from 8 to 16 egg yolks and 1 to 1 ¼ cups (200 to 250 g) sugar for every 4 cups (1 l) of milk. Here, the sugar is reduced because the marmalade already contains sugar. ❧

$\mathscr{P}$rincess Diana's Favorite Fish

*Renowned for her beauty and elegance, Princess Diana also loved fine food—
and if ever there was a mishap of any kind she invariably took it in good
spirits. On the frequent occasions when she dined at the Embassy, her favorite
dish was one of James's great specialties—delicately flavored sea bass, braised,
stuffed, or flambéed, perhaps, and served on a silver platter.*

*A dish fit for a princess. But it was at a simpler occasion, a luncheon in the
Salon Bleu, that the mishap in question occurred. Some twenty guests had been
invited to a charity lunch; on the menu were sausages made with potato and
cheese, served with a tomato sauce. Princess Diana was wearing a dazzling
jacket in blue raw silk. As Ben, the butler, offered her the dish, he noticed that
there was a splash of tomato sauce on the elbow of her jacket.*

*To allow the Princess to go through the day with a large red stain on one sleeve
was unthinkable. What was to be done? Unflappable as ever, Ben called the
Princess's dresser, who slipped into the room, whisked away the stained jacket,
and replaced it with a fresh one. The incident was over before anyone had
even noticed. Except for the ambassador's wife, that is, who had observed the
whole scene as it unfolded and recalls to this day her own consternation—
immaculately concealed, naturally.*

Sea Bass Braised in Champagne

Serves 8

INGREDIENTS

1 sea bass weighing 4 ½ lb. (2 kg)	2 teaspoons cornstarch
1 medium carrot (3 oz./80 g)	2 cups (500 ml) fish fumet
3 ½ oz. (100 g) button mushrooms	2 cups (500 ml) dry champagne
2 large shallots	Salt
5 ½ tablespoons (80 g) butter	Freshly ground white pepper

For the garnish

2 large, unblemished cucumbers	1 heaping tablespoon thick crème fraîche
¾ cup (200 ml) champagne	2 heaping tablespoons chopped chives
10 oz. (300 g) smoked salmon	Small bunch of parsley

For the sauce

7 tablespoons (3 ½ oz./100 g) butter	Juice of ½ lemon
5 egg yolks	Cayenne pepper

Prepare the sea bass: With a heavy knife, scrape the fish from the head to the tail to remove the scales. Cut off the fins with a pair of scissors. Leave the tail whole. With a knife and a pair of scissors, remove the gills. Use this opening to insert the hook of a skimmer to gut the fish. Repeat several times until all the innards are removed. Wash the inside of the fish under cold running water. This procedure allows the belly of the sea bass to remain intact and makes for an attractive presentation.

Lightly oil the rack of a fish kettle and place the sea bass on it.

Preheat the oven to 375°F (190°C). Peel the carrot and cut it into small dice. Clean the mushrooms and cut them into small dice. Press them in a cloth to remove any excess water. Peel the shallots and chop them very finely. Heat the butter in a sauté pan and sauté the carrot, mushrooms, and shallots until they are a light golden color. Dissolve the cornstarch with the fish fumet and pour it into the sauté pan. Add the champagne and season with salt and pepper, but only lightly, as the liquid will reduce. Pour it all into the fish kettle, taking care not to wet the fish at this stage, and place in the oven without the lid. Cook for 35 minutes, basting the fish with the cooking liquid as often as possible. Once you have removed the fish from the oven, cover it with the lid and keep in a warm place so that the poaching can continue.

Meanwhile, prepare the garnish: Wash the cucumbers. With a cannelle knife, make grooves down their length and cut them into 1-inch (2.5 cm) pieces. With a teaspoon or small scoop, make small balls, hollowing out the cucumber pieces to make small "cases." Arrange them side by side in a sauté pan and pour in the champagne. Season lightly with salt. Bring to a boil, remove immediately from direct heat, cover with the lid, and let poach. The cucumbers must not soften too much or they will lose their shape.

Cut the smoked salmon into small dice. Combine with the crème fraîche, half the chives, and the pepper. There is no need to season with salt as the smoked salmon is sufficiently salty.

For the sauce: Remove the sea bass, still on its rack, from the fish kettle. Pour the cooking liquid into a saucepan. Return the fish to the fish kettle and cover with the lid. Reduce the cooking liquid over high heat until 1 cup (250 ml) remains. In a small heavy-bottomed saucepan, melt the butter. Let rest for a few minutes until the milk solids fall to the bottom of the saucepan. Pour 1 ½ inches (3 cm) water into a metal dish and bring to a simmer. Place the egg yolks and 5 tablespoons water in a small heavy-bottomed saucepan. Place the saucepan in the simmering water and whisk the egg yolks continuously until they form a foamy, hot cream. It must not be boiling hot, otherwise the egg yolks will cook too quickly and become grainy. Whisk more gently, gradually adding the melted butter, but not the milk solids. Add the lemon juice and a small pinch of Cayenne pepper. Still whisking gently, incorporate the reduced cooking liquid.

To serve: Drain the cucumber "cases" and fill them with the smoked salmon and cream mixture. Keep them in a warm place to heat the salmon just slightly.* Remove the sea bass from the fish kettle, take off the skin with a small knife, and then scrape off the brown flesh, which is the fatty part of the fish. Slide the sea bass onto a platter. Arrange the cucumber "cases" around it. Drizzle a little sauce over the fish and sprinkle with the remaining chives. Place the bunch of parsley at the opening of the gills. Serve the remaining sauce in a sauce dish. Sometimes I alternate baby potatoes or carrots with the cucumbers and I add small puff pastry crescents known as *fleurons*.

If you don't have a fish kettle, cook the sea bass in slices or pieces taken from the fillet. Cook them for no longer than 4 minutes over low heat and finish cooking them for another 4 minutes in the oven. If you use this method, make the base of the sauce ahead of time using the head and bones of the fish. ❧

* I find that when smoked salmon is overheated, it loses its distinctive flavor.

$\mathcal{T}$he Maestro and La Belle Bernadette

Yehudi Menuhin was a regular guest at the Embassy. Every time he gave a concert in Paris he and his wife would stay at the Ambassador's Residence, which was like a second home to them. For his sixtieth birthday a grand dinner was given in his honor, but generally the great violinist, who would be met on the entrance stairs by the ambassador, lived in relatively simple style. Discreet and thoughtful, he never failed to send a thank-you note to James after a particularly fine meal. His favorite dish was a dessert: sorbet à la poire Williamine. This was not just any sorbet, however. This was a sorbet made with fresh pears, poached in a vanilla syrup, molded into a pear shape in a balloon, served on a genoise sponge, and decorated with a stem made from spun sugar and two almond paste leaves.

Yehudi Menuhin's passion for pears was shared by another of the Embassy's distinguished guests—Bernadette Chirac. Usually she would come on her own, without her husband, President Jacques Chirac, which meant that the occasion could be less formal. For the State Dinner given for the Queen on the eve of her departure from Paris in 2004, for instance, instead of being seated around the banqueting table, guests were placed at round tables for eight set out in the ballroom. The menu that evening featured a moelleux au chocolat chaud (a rich chocolate cake served warm) with vanilla ice cream, but Bernadette Chirac's favorite dessert was pear sorbet. The first time she tasted it at the Embassy she loved it so much that she went straight back to the Elysée Palace and asked the chef to get the recipe. Ever since, the dessert has been known as "Sorbet Belle Bernadette."

FACING PAGE *American violinist Yehudi Menuhin (1916–1999), playing at the Paris Opera in February 1967 and his thank-you note to Chef James following his visit to the British Embassy in 1976.*

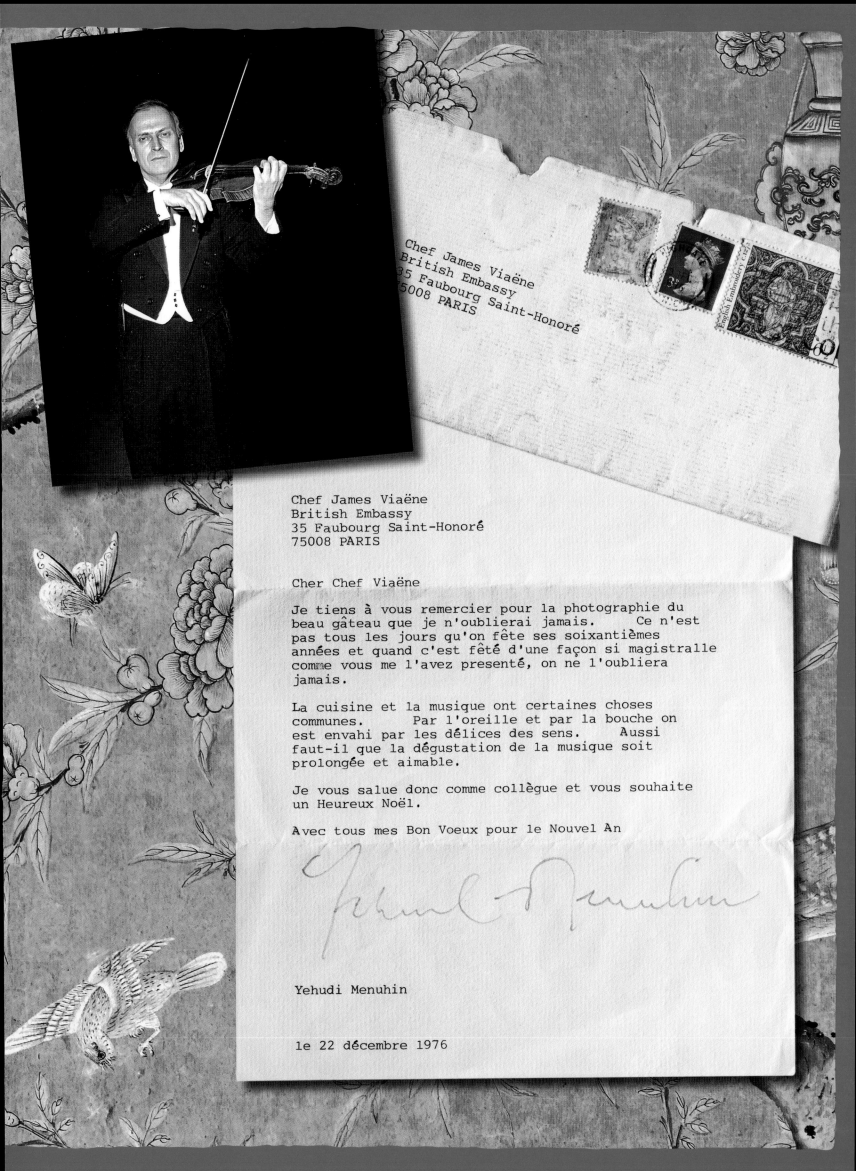

Chef James Viaëne
British Embassy
35 Faubourg Saint-Honoré
75008 PARIS

Cher Chef Viaëne

Je tiens à vous remercier pour la photographie du
beau gâteau que je n'oublierai jamais.   Ce n'est
pas tous les jours qu'on fête ses soixantièmes
années et quand c'est fêté d'une façon si magistralle
comme vous me l'avez présenté, on ne l'oubliera
jamais.

La cuisine et la musique ont certaines choses
communes.   Par l'oreille et par la bouche on
est envahi par les délices des sens.   Aussi
faut-il que la dégustation de la musique soit
prolongée et aimable.

Je vous salue donc comme collègue et vous souhaite
un Heureux Noël.

Avec tous mes Bon Voeux pour le Nouvel An

Yehudi Menuhin

le 22 décembre 1976

Sorbet Belle Bernadette

Serves 8 or more

Prepare a day ahead

INGREDIENTS

3 cups (750 ml) water	Juice of ½ lemon
1 ¼ cups (250 g) sugar	8 large pears, preferably Bartlett (Williams)
½ vanilla bean, slit lengthwise	

For the decoration

7 oz. (200 g) almond paste	1 ¼ cups (300 ml) water
Coffee extract or cocoa powder	¼ cup (2 oz./50 g) sugar
Red, green, and yellow food coloring	1 round genoise sponge, diameter about 6 inches (15 cm)

For the coulis

1 ½ lb. (750 g) pears, preferably Bartlett (Williams)	Juice of 1 lemon
1 cup plus 3 tablespoons (8 oz./225 g) sugar	A little Williamine liqueur

SPECIAL EQUIPMENT

A soft pastry brush, a pastry bag fitted with a small, plain tip, and a balloon, well washed and dried.

A day ahead, make the sorbet: Pour the water into a medium heavy-bottomed saucepan and add the sugar and the slit vanilla bean. Heat until the syrup just begins to boil. Remove from heat and add the lemon juice. Peel and core the pears. Cut them into small cubes. As you cut them, drop them into the syrup so that they do not go brown. Return the saucepan to the heat and bring back to a boil. Cook for no longer than 3 to 4 minutes.

Remove the vanilla bean. With a slotted spoon, remove the pieces of pear and process with ¾ cup (200 ml) of the syrup until very smooth to make the most delicate coulis possible. Strain through a fine-mesh sieve and let cool.

Pour the mixture into an ice cream maker and proceed according to the manufacturer's directions. If you don't have an ice cream maker, pour the mixture into a bowl and freeze, stirring from time to time, until it reaches the consistency of a sorbet.

Transfer the sorbet to a piping bag and pipe it into the balloon until it is almost full. Close the neck of the balloon with kitchen twine, leaving enough to hang it, and hang it in the freezer so that it takes the shape of a pear. Let harden.

For the decoration: color a knob of almond paste with a few drops of coffee extract or a little cocoa powder. Shape it into the stem of the pear.

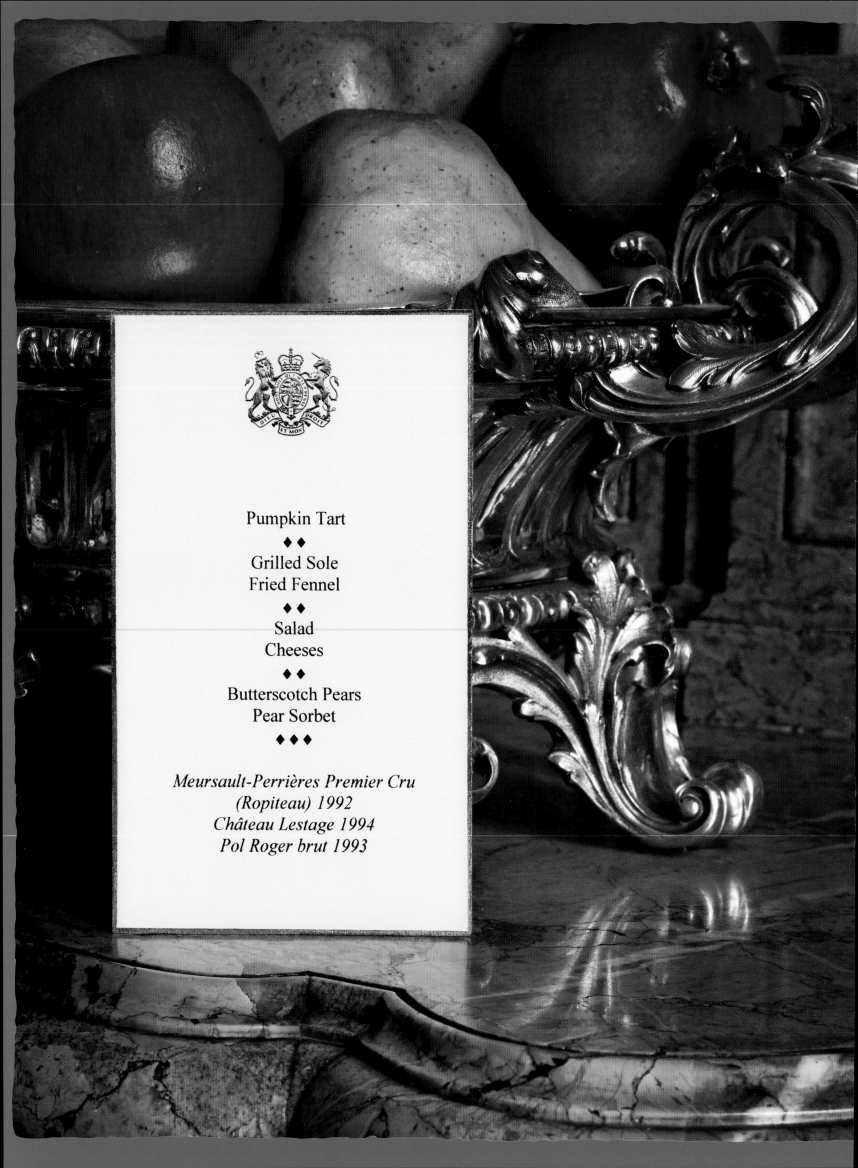

Pumpkin Tart
◆ ◆
Grilled Sole
Fried Fennel
◆ ◆
Salad
Cheeses
◆ ◆
Butterscotch Pears
Pear Sorbet
◆ ◆ ◆

Meursault-Perrières Premier Cru
(Ropiteau) 1992
Château Lestage 1994
Pol Roger brut 1993

Color the remaining almond paste with a few drop of green coloring. Roll out some of it very thinly (less than ⅛ inch or 2 mm) and cut out leaves. This will be easiest if you have a small cutter. With the back of a small knife, draw the veins of the leaves.

Divide the remaining green almond paste into five pieces. Flatten each one with the palm of your hand to different thicknesses and push each piece through a sieve, still pressing with the palm of your hand. The almond paste will now look like moss.

Place the stem, leaves, and moss (use a knife to pick up the moss) on parchment paper and let dry overnight.

The following day, make the coulis to accompany the sorbet: Peel and core the pears. Cut them into pieces and place them in a medium heavy-bottomed saucepan. Add the sugar. Cook over low heat for about 15 minutes, until the pieces fall apart. Blend with the lemon juice and strain through a fine-mesh sieve. Transfer to an airtight container and chill for at least 3 hours.

To make the colors to decorate the pear-shaped sorbet, combine 1 ¼ cups (300 ml) water with ¼ cup (2 oz./50 g) superfine sugar. Divide the sugar and water mixture into three parts. Carefully color one part red, one part green, and the third part yellow. Add the food coloring drop by drop, as the colors should not be too bright.

Place the balloon containing the sorbet onto a plate and, using a small pair of scissors, cut open the balloon and carefully remove the pear-shaped sorbet. With a brush, color the pear yellow. Then, working from the base up, color some parts green and others red so that the sorbet looks like a red Bartlett pear.

Place the round of genoise sponge on the serving dish and carefully transfer the pear onto it. Make a small indentation at the top of the pear and stick in the stem. Add the leaves and place the moss around the base of the pear.

Add a little Williamine liqueur to the coulis, pour it into a sauce dish, and serve it with the sorbet. ❧

Perfection in Simplicity

CHEFS IN PRIVATE HOUSEHOLDS MUST HAVE A PROFOUND KNOWLEDGE OF CUISINE AND A BROAD repertoire. A select handful of sublime dishes is not enough: these chefs must be able to put together an entire menu. Their skill lies in offering a day-to-day cuisine that is light, refined, and immaculate. This at least is the belief of the current president of the Club des Cent, Jean Solanet. Perfection in simplicity is indisputably the quality that he most admires, with the emphasis on the quality of the products, the cooking, and the seasonings—and emphatically not on over-erudite research.

Excelling in the vanishing art of making *pommes soufflées* and cooking a rack of lamb to perfection are a couple of the distinguishing marks of a great chef such as James. But there are others: a truly great chef must also be able to rise to the challenge of the most unexpected demands, and must understand the codes that govern individual tastes and beliefs. In a career spanning fifty-eight years, James has garnered a wealth of experience, along with a peerless mastery of the fads and foibles, habits and preferences of high society, from the Duke of Windsor's breakfast croquettes to the modest portions preferred by the Queen, or the Chief Rabbi's carp. In the Michel David-Weill household, very little red meat was eaten; at the Wildensteins' home, braised meat was preferred and offal was abhorred; in observant Jewish households, care must be taken to keep eggs and chicken apart, as mother and offspring must never be consumed on the same day; and those of a certain age often prefer traditional recipes that take them back to the days of their youth.

But his finest hour came one evening when the Duchess of Windsor was a guest at the British Embassy and refused to eat the dessert, which was not to her taste. In no time at all, James had not only whipped up one of her favorite dishes, an individual orange soufflé served in the orange skin, but had also contrived to have it served to her even before the butler had finished serving the other guests. Great art indeed, but also great tact and sensitivity.

Only the Finest Suppliers

THE CHOICE OF SUPPLIERS IS ESSENTIAL IN ENSURING ABSOLUTE QUALITY AT REASONABLE PRICES. FOR many years Les Halles was the market where chefs and restaurateurs would go to bargain hard for crates of vegetables, sides of meat, and live fish or whitebait. Its only rival was the market on rue des Belles-Feuilles in the sixteenth arrondissement, highly valued by chefs from wealthy private households for the quality of its suppliers, including Lahoche for vegetables and "Au poulet de Bresse" for poultry. After the departure of Les Halles for Rungis, James drew up a new list of suppliers, most of them French. But there are some areas—particularly cheeses—where the Embassy has an important image to maintain, and where products are still imported from Britain.

Directing the kitchen's commis chefs is another aspect of the chef's mission, and one of essential importance. James recalls his own apprenticeship: "When I started out in London, the chef would say 'Do this, do that,' but he would never reveal the whole recipe and wouldn't even let us see the menu book. In my bedroom at night I would try to write them down from memory so I could do them again, but it never worked." And then there was his habit of giving deliberately skimpy instructions and the wrong proportions (too much butter, say, or not enough). Master chefs in those days guarded their secrets jealously. But for James there was no question of following the same system that he had endured. He prefers a lighter touch: "Some chefs are very controlling, but not me. I give my commis chefs a plan and tell them to work it out for themselves. I teach them to use their initiative."

James would also take the responsibility for the occasional blunder, such as a recipe containing carrot, pumpkin, and cilantro for which one of the commis chefs grated the carrots far too coarsely, with disastrous results. Conversely, beginners' mistakes can often produce successful new recipes. *Boeuf gros sel*, for instance, came about when a commis chef by mistake added kosher instead of fine salt to the recipe, with results that were so convincing that the recipe was adopted forthwith.

Fish and Chips

If there is an arbiter of French gastronomic excellence, it has to be the Club des Cent, the ultra-exclusive circle of a hundred men (and they are all men)— captains of business and industry, bankers, lawyers, actors, journalists, personalities—who every Thursday sit down together to an outstanding meal organized by one of their number. Founded in 1912, in the early days of motor touring, the Club's original purpose was to point its members in the direction of the best restaurants they might find en route. Over the years, it developed into the holy of holies of French gourmets, championing the excellence of French cuisine, hailing its finest chefs and best restaurants. To be admitted as a member is a privilege, and one that must be earned by sitting a rigorous examination on matters culinary. James is one of the chefs who is most appreciated by members of the Club des Cent, known as "centenaires." As guests of the British Embassy on various occasions, many of them had already had the opportunity to sample the perfection of its cuisine, and the idea of a meal there dedicated to the Club was one of their dreams. Thus it was that, on June 30, 2011, the Thursday lunch of the Club des Cent was held at the Embassy. For the occasion, they asked James to make the most democratic of appetizers: fish and chips. The origins of fish and chips are British. From the eighteenth century, London street-sellers did a brisk trade in portions of fried fish served with fried potatoes and, occasionally, mushy peas, all wrapped in newspaper. Easy to eat on the spot or to take home, fish and chips spread around the globe, as far as Australia and New Zealand, then back to North America, Belgium, and Holland.

*In France, it was "pommes Pont Neuf" that gained popular approval.
Sold on the pont Neuf to Parisians on their way back from the market in
the Marais, these fried potatoes, roughly cut into chunky triangular
shapes, were also known as "pommes coin de rue," or "street-corner chips."
In James's view any fish can be used for fish and chips, but, all the same,
he advises using cod. In order to preserve the authenticity of the dish while
also creating an elegant presentation, he makes miniature paper cones
and fills each of them with a slender goujon of fish and a couple of chips;
he then clips the filled cones around the edge of the plate to make ideal
canapés for cocktails or aperitifs. They certainly have a vote of confidence
from Jean Solanet, president of the Club des Cent. Faced with the all the
culinary excesses and outlandish experiments of recent years, he appreciates
simple, classic cuisine all the more, using only the finest ingredients.
A return to basics, par excellence.*

ABOVE *The Club des Cent meeting for their weekly
meal at 4, avenue Hoche in Paris, c. 1923.*

145

FISH AND CHIPS

This favorite British dish was traditionally served in newspaper cones. Lady Jay, the wife of one of the ambassadors, asked me if I could make a small version of the dish to serve at receptions. I was delighted with the idea and it was very popular when I made it. The only problem is that newspaper does not go very well with food. So I hit on the idea of photocopying a page of a newspaper (a British one, of course) onto one side of sheets of white paper.

Makes 16 cones

INGREDIENTS

¼ cake (⅕ oz./5 g) fresh yeast	3 to 4 potatoes
1 ¼ cups (300 ml) warm water	Oil for frying
2 cups (7 oz./200 g) all-purpose flour	2 cod fillets
2 tablespoons olive oil	2 egg whites
1 teaspoon (5 g) salt	16 photocopies of a British newspaper to serve

For the batter: Crumble the yeast into the water. Pour the flour into a mixing bowl. Make a well in the center and pour in the diluted yeast, the oil, and then the salt. Mix briskly to combine. Cover and let the batter rise for 2 hours in a warm place, until almost doubled in volume.

Meanwhile, prepare the paper cones. Cut sixteen 6 ½-inch (16 cm) disks from the photocopies and make a 3-inch (8 cm) incision with a pair of scissors to the center of each disk. Slip the two sides together to form cones, placing the white part inside. Stick or staple them together to hold the shape.

Heat the frying oil to 400°F (200°C). Peel the potatoes and cut them into chips. Cut them again to make mini-chips. Cut the cod fillets to the same size. Drop the potatoes into the hot oil and cook until golden. Drain on paper towel. Keep them hot and dry in a warm place, for example, an oven at 200°F (100°C).

Beat the egg whites until firm and fold them carefully into the batter. With a small skewer, dip the cod fillets into the batter and then drop them into the hot oil. Let them color nicely, then drain on paper towel.

Fill each paper cone with three mini chips and three pieces of fried cod. Serve immediately.

Originally, these fish and chips were served accompanied by puréed split peas. This pulse must be soaked for 8 hours before it is cooked. When the split peas are boiled and puréed, add enough cream to give the consistency of a coulis. Serve it in small ramekins. 🍂

How Far is Too Far?

ONE OF THE CHALLENGES FACING CONTEMPORARY CUISINE IS THE QUESTION OF HOW TO DEVELOP new techniques and practices while at the same time preserving the principles of the great tradition of classic cuisine. With his invention of "molecular gastronomy," the Spanish chef Ferran Adrià started a veritable revolution, introducing chemical processes into the kitchens at his restaurant El Bulli (now closed) in order to transform the ingredients he used. The results were impossible to ignore. His dried raspberries topped with a lavender pistil were breathtaking, Jean Solanet acknowledges, but is Ferran Adrià really a chef? Even Adrià himself admits that he has his doubts.

In the view of Hélène David-Weill, who dismisses all forms of excess, such fads are simply a form of snobbery: whether in art, couture, or cooking, the desire to be creative and cutting-edge at all costs can lead to all sorts of nonsense, with a tendency to forget that fashion is meant to be worn and cuisine to be eaten! One of her worst experiences was truffle ice cream with a pumpkin sauce, which she describes as simply inedible.

James's approach is to balance the two, to add touches of modernity to a basic repertoire of recognized classics. As early as the 1960s, he surprised Madame Badrutt, wife of the owner of the Palace Hotel in Saint-Moritz, with his suggestion for fillets of sole with a curry sauce, a novel combination for the period. "Do you really think so?" was her puzzled response. But by the following day, having sought the advice of the hotel chef, she was convinced.

Still today, James likes to innovate. He enjoys certain combinations of sweet and sour, marrying carrots with oranges and offering some dishes with citrus accompaniments; he likes to serve beetroot mousse flavored with the zest of an orange, apple turnovers with a hint of zucchini, and sweet pumpkin soufflés. But he is careful never to go too far.

"James always maintains a happy medium, executing the great classics to perfection and avoiding the pitfalls of nouvelle cuisine," is Jean Solanet's admiring verdict. His crown roasts of lamb are spectacular and perfectly cooked, but he never indulges in excessive complications. Like the President of the Club des Cent, James is convinced that crowding ten different flavors and four different cooking techniques on to a single plate is not a sign of great cooking, but rather a recipe for "total disaster."

148

SADDLE OF SALT MARSH WELSH LAMB

Serves 6

INGREDIENTS

4 large floury potatoes	1 carrot
Olive oil	1 onion
1 sprig fresh thyme	Zest of 1 lemon
Piment d'Espelette	4 tablespoons (60 g) butter, divided
Oil for frying	1 bay leaf, crumbled
18 baby carrots with greens remaining	2 cups (500 ml) lamb stock
18 baby turnips with greens remaining	1 tablespoon redcurrant jelly
1 ½ lb. (700 g) garden peas	2 tablespoons sugar
2 saddles of lamb, 2 ¼ lb. (1 kg) apiece,	Salt
each trimmed and tied (reserve the trimmings)	Freshly ground pepper
1 to 2 tablespoons honey	A bunch of watercress to serve

Peel the potatoes. Using a peeler, cut them into 1-inch (2.5 cm) wide ribbons, starting at the top and rotating the potato as you would for an apple. Place the ribbons in a mixing bowl, drizzle with a little olive oil, add 1 sprig thyme, and sprinkle with a pinch of *piment d'Espelette*. Marinate for 1 hour. Roll up the potato ribbons and hold them in place with a toothpick or small wooden skewer. Heat the frying oil to 350°F (180°C), drop in the potato ribbons, and fry until very crisp. Drain them, remove the toothpicks, season with salt, and transfer to a dish. This part of the dish may be made well ahead of time.

Peel the baby carrots and turnips and trim their greens to just over 1 inch (3 cm). Shell the peas.

Preheat the oven to 400°F (200°C). With a small, sharp knife, make criss-cross incisions in the fat covering the saddles. Brush with a thin layer of honey. Season lightly with salt and freshly ground pepper. Peel and slice the carrot. Peel the onion and cut it into 6. Cut the lemon zest into fine julienne slices.

In a roasting pan, brown the meat trimmings, carrot slices, and pieces of onion with 1 ½ tablespoons (20 g) butter. Add the crumbled bay leaf and lemon zest and season with pepper.

Place the saddles of lamb on this bed and season with salt. Roast for 20 minutes, turning the meat every 5 minutes. When it is done, remove from the dish and keep warm, covered with foil or parchment paper.

Pour the lamb stock into the cooking dish and cook for 15 minutes. Strain the liquid into a small saucepan and add the redcurrant jelly. Reduce by half.

Meanwhile, cook the baby carrots and turnips for a few minutes in boiling salted water. They should retain their crunch. Cook the peas separately in boiling salted water.

Arrange the carrots in a dish and brush them with 1 ½ tablespoons (20 g) melted butter.

Melt the remaining (20 g) butter in a pan large enough to hold the turnips in a single layer. Sprinkle the sugar into the butter and arrange the turnips upright in the pan so that the stalks stay intact. Let caramelize over low heat.

Remove the fillets from the saddles, ensuring that there are two grooves on each saddle. Cut angled slices, each saddle in the opposite direction. Return the fillet slices to the groove so that they look like a sheaf of corn.

Place the saddles of lamb on the serving platter with a bunch of watercress in the center. Surround them with the peas. Then alternate three overlapping carrots with three turnips all around the platter. Place the potato ribbons together between the saddles of lamb and the carrot and turnip garnish. Brush the food with a little sauce so that it is shiny and pour the remaining sauce into a dish to serve on the side.

Conversation, Elegance, and Gourmet Dining

LADIES' LUNCHES

In post-war Paris, when the art of conversation was still cultivated with care,
Lady Diana Cooper, wife of Ambassador Duff Cooper, would invite
her friends Edmonde Charles-Roux, Louise de Vilmorin,
and Baroness Philippe de Rothschild to the residence in order to exchange
news and ideas over afternoon tea. Very soon, these teatime gatherings
moved to lunchtime. Whether they were held in embassies, in order to
introduce ladies newly arrived from abroad to the customs of the country,
or at the homes of society hostesses, with a prominent personality as guest of
honor, these ladies' luncheons were to flourish for several decades.
According to Maryvonne Pinault, hostess of the most elegant ladies'
luncheons in Paris, a successful occasion requires meticulous planning.
The golden rule is that they must bring together women of different
backgrounds who are able to share their experiences, ensuring that guests
will always leave having made new acquaintances. Other essentials are
that there should be no more than eight guests, in order to encourage ease of
conversation, and that a full menu should be served. Madame Pinault serves
an appetizer, followed by a main course of white meat or fish, an obligatory
cheese course in order to promote French specialties, and a light dessert.
Her table settings, meanwhile, are the quintessence of French elegance,
with Sèvres porcelain, eighteenth-century glasses (with the exception of the
wine glasses selected to reveal the full magnificence of the great Bordeaux
vintages), and flowers chosen to complement the dinner service or according
to the season. Few hostesses can vie with such perfection. Over the years,
domestic arrangements have become more restricted, and more and more
young women are choosing to follow professional careers. Limitations of
means and time have meant that ladies' lunches have moved out of private
houses and into restaurants; some lunch meetings have even metamorphosed
into associations. After Monique Taittinger, who used to entertain
at Le Grand Véfour, in the early years of this century Monique Raimond
began a monthly ladies' literary lunch at Maxim's in Paris, whith an

author invited to talk about his or her latest book—a stylish marriage of culture, elegance, and gourmet food. In today's working environment, where businesswomen prefer light lunches on the go, diplomatic habits too have evolved away from formal decorum and toward simplicity. The old world and the new now coexist together. As well as the traditional ladies' lunches, there are now lunches organized around an author or theme, as well as lunches for "girlfriends," which couldn't be simpler or less stuffy. Lady Westmacott, for instance, used to enjoy sharing James's delicious steak tartare, French fries, and béarnaise sauce with her friends Valérie Hortefeux and Sophie Dumenil: the ultimate in simplicity, which only a few years ago would have been simply unthinkable!

ABOVE *Lady Diana Cooper, photographed by Cecil Beaton in the Salon Jaune of the British Ambassador's Residence in Paris, December 4, 1944.*

STEAK TARTARE

Steak tartare is a dish said to have originated among the Cossack Tartars living in what is now Ukraine. The author Jules Verne gives a description of it in his novel Michel Strogoff. *It has become a specialty at the restaurant named for Jules Verne, on the second floor of the Eiffel Tower. Here is my version of steak tartare as I served it at the British Embassy in Paris.*

Serves 8

INGREDIENTS

2 ½ lb. (1.15 kg) beef (rib steak, tenderloin, or Porterhouse steak)
2 oz. (50 g) capers
2 oz. (50 g) gherkins
2 oz. (50 g) white onions
1 tablespoon Dijon mustard
2 tablespoons tomato ketchup

2 teaspoons Worcestershire sauce
A few drops Tabasco sauce
1 heaping tablespoon fine sea salt
5 grinds of the pepper mill
8 eggs
A few leaves of tarragon and capers for garnish
Béarnaise sauce (see page 159)

With a very sharp knife, cut the beef into ⅛-inch (4 mm) slices, then cut these slices into ⅛-inch (4 mm) strips. Next, cut the strips into ⅛-inch (4 mm) dice. Transfer them to a large mixing bowl. Cover and chill while you prepare the accompanying ingredients. The meat should turn red.

Chop the capers and dice the gherkins finely. Peel and dice the onions finely.

Add the capers, gherkins, and onions to the meat. Add the mustard, tomato ketchup, Worcestershire sauce, Tabasco, salt, and pepper. Stir carefully to combine. Let the meat macerate in the refrigerator for no more than 20 to 30 minutes.

Just before serving, divide the meat into 8 equal portions, placing each one on a plate. With the back of a spoon, make a little hollow in the center of the mound. Separate the eggs one by one, placing a yolk in the hollow over the meat (you will need the yolks only; reserve the whites for another recipe). Garnish each plate with a few tarragon leaves and whole capers. Serve with the Béarnaise sauce on the side.

Each guest uses his fork to mix the egg yolk into the meat and adds a spoonful of sauce. At the Embassy, we serve steak tartare with French fries.

Chefs have invented all sorts of variations on this recipe, using other types of meat, game, fish, or scallops, with delicious results. Some prefer to chop the meat finely, while others cut it into thin strips.

To make steak tartare, I recommend rib steak, rump steak, Porterhouse, or sirloin— all tender, tasty cuts, that are, with the exception of the rib steak (entrecote), lean. ❧

BÉARNAISE SAUCE

INGREDIENTS

1 small bunch tarragon
4 black peppercorns
2 tablespoons white wine vinegar
4 tablespoons dry white wine

1 generous pinch sugar
5 eggs
2 tablespoons (30 g) butter, room temperature
Salt and freshly ground pepper

Pick the tarragon leaves off the stalks and chop them. Roughly crush the peppercorns. In a small saucepan, place half the chopped tarragon, peppercorns, white wine vinegar, white wine, and sugar (this reduces the acidity of the sauce). Bring to a boil. Reduce the heat to low, and simmer, uncovered, until all the liquid has evaporated.

Meanwhile, separate the eggs, breaking at least one shell cleanly in half. You will need the yolks only; reserve the whites for another recipe. Set aside at least one half eggshell.

Transfer the reduction to a mixing bowl and keep warm. Pour in the egg yolks and 5 half eggshells-worth of cold water. Pour hot, not boiling, water into a bain-marie and set the mixing bowl over it. With a small whisk, whip the egg yolks, lifting well to incorporate as much air as possible, until the mixture forms a hot mousse. As you work, make sure that the water in the bain-marie does not boil, because the heat would curdle the egg yolks.

Dice the butter and gradually whisk it in. Incorporate the remaining tarragon. Adjust the seasoning. Keep the sauce warm over a bain-marie until needed. ❧

British Specialties

Who knew? While France prides itself on its four hundred or so different
varieties of cheese, Britain quietly boasts almost as many. There are even
cheeses made on the royal estates, so that the Queen can take them with her
on state visits as gifts for her hosts. Stilton, still made according to
the traditional technique, and cheddar in all its many varieties are among
the most widely available. But alongside these there are many less familiar cheeses,
made from ewes' milk, cows' milk or goats' milk, that are equally rich and delicious.
They include Berkswell from the Midlands, made from ewes' milk
and matured for four months; extra-mature Black Bomber Cheddar
from Snowdonia, a particular favorite of Penelope Fillon, wife of the former
French Prime Minister; Tunworth, a soft camembert-style cheese from Hampshire;
Tymsboro goats'-milk cheese from Somerset; and Welsh Gorwydd Caerphilly.
Lady Jay, went out of her way to make British cheeses better known in France, and
ever since her time a selection of some twenty of them have been a regular feature at
the ambassador's table. Only one is never seen, for fear that it might cause offence to
those of a delicate constitution because of its name: Stinking Bishop! When it comes
to serving the cheeses, the old traditional ways and modern habits take it in turns,
depending on the occasion. For Christmas dinner tradition prevails, and Stilton is
always served after the Christmas pudding, accompanied by a glass of vintage port.
But the old way of serving Stilton—slicing the top off a whole truckle, boring holes
in it, feeding it with port over a couple of weeks, and then spooning it out—
is one custom that has been dropped. Nowadays, concerns for healthy eating have
seen the cheese course banished from most lunch tables, but this does not deter James
from recommending a starter of Stilton or Berkswell with a green salad,
a little celery, a few walnuts, and sliced pears. At the dinner table, the cheese course
is restored to its rightful place, served before dessert and accompanied by Carr's
water biscuits, oatcakes, and walnut bread. And if the ambassador becomes aware
that any of his guests particularly enjoys British cheese, he will often make sure
they are given one of these specialties to take home with them.

The English Breakfast

FROM HEARTY TO HEALTHY

"To eat well in England, you should have breakfast three times a day":
W. Somerset Maugham's famous advice sums up the special place
held by English breakfast. What are the origins of the English breakfast?
No one really knows. Well before tea arrived on British shores from China,
in the seventeenth century, the English enjoyed breaking their fast (hence the
name) with a substantial morning meal of bread and beef. Imports of Irish pork
in the eighteenth century led to bacon becoming more freely available,
a tradition that continues to this day, with an annual consumption of
450,000 tons, plus another 5,000 tons of sausages. Black pudding,
that other essential ingredient, arrived in Britain from mainland Europe,
probably brought by monks. By the nineteenth century the magic ingredients
of the "full English breakfast"—eggs and bacon, porridge, and toast and
marmalade, all washed down with a pot of tea—had finally come together.
It can also feature scrambled eggs with smoked salmon,
or kedgeree (composed of fish, rice, and hard-boiled eggs),
the recipe for which was brought back from India by British officers.
Times change, and habits with them. Sir Christopher Soames requested an
electric toaster on his breakfast table, to ensure his toast was warm,
and in these more health-conscious times ambassadors prefer a lighter breakfast
of cereal, muesli, and fruit (Sir Ewen Fergusson was particularly fond
of papaya). The "full English" breakfast is now served only when there are
guests, or at working breakfasts. But James still remembers with nostalgia
those not-so-distant days when breakfast would be served up with the dawn,
at five or six in the morning, after a grand ball. At that time in the morning,
a good hearty kedgeree was absolutely de rigueur.

Afternoon Tea
A HALLOWED TRADITION

*It was the Portuguese princess, Catherine of Braganza who introduced
tea to Britain when she came to marry Charles II in 1662. For many years
this beverage from China remained the preserve of wealthy aristocrats,
until it dropped in price during the nineteenth century. Tea drinking then
became so widespread that the rhythm of the British day was dictated by
the times when people stopped for a cup of tea, from first thing on waking to last
thing at night, via breakfast, morning tea, and afternoon tea. Afternoon tea
was introduced in about 1840 by the young Duchess of Bedford,
lady-in-waiting to the equally young Queen Victoria, as a snack to bridge
the gap between luncheon—then a light meal taken early—and dinner.
The refreshment that she devised for a few lady friends, consisting of tea
and cakes, proved such a success that it became a national institution.
For authentic afternoon tea as served at the Embassy,
James advises the strict observation of the following golden rules:
☙ although any type of tea is acceptable, the Embassy prefers traditional Earl Grey;
☙ lemon meringue tartlets are the perfect accompaniment;
☙ scones should be served with strawberry jam and clotted cream;
☙ lemon cake (a traditional Victoria sponge filled with lemon curd) is a favorite;
☙ cucumber and egg sandwiches may be flavored with lightly seasoned
soft cheese, but pungent flavorings such as chives, tarragon, or garlic
should be avoided.*

LEMON CAKE

*There are numerous versions of this famous cake. Here is mine, simple and always
a great hit with the guests at the Embassy. Even a friend who is not fond of lemon thinks
it's delicious, and many people have asked me for my recipe.*

Serves 8

INGREDIENTS

6 unsprayed or organic lemons	6 eggs
1 ½ cups (10 ½ oz./300 g) sugar	7 tablespoons (3 ½ oz./100 g) butter
2 teaspoons cornstarch	

For the sponge

2 unsprayed or organic lemons	1 ¾ cups (6 oz./170 g) all-purpose flour
1 ½ sticks (6 oz./170 g) unsalted butter	1 pinch baking powder
Scant cup (6 oz./170 g) sugar	3 large eggs
1 small pinch vanilla powder	
or 1 teaspoon pure vanilla extract*	

For the syrup

2 lemons	2 tablespoons water
Scant ⅔ cup (4 ¼ oz./120 g) sugar	

For dusting

Confectioners' sugar

For the lemon curd: Wash 2 of the 6 lemons, dry them, and grate the zest finely. Squeeze the
6 lemons and strain the juice. Pour it into a medium heavy-bottomed saucepan with the sugar, lemon
zest, and cornstarch. Begin cooking over low heat. Lightly beat the eggs. When the sugar has melted,
add the eggs, stirring constantly so that the mixture does not stick. When it has thickened, stir in the
butter. Continue stirring until it has melted, remove from heat, and let cool. You can keep the lemon
curd in an airtight container in the refrigerator for several weeks.

    For the sponge: Preheat the oven to 375°F (190°C). Butter a 6-inch (15 cm) cake pan 4 inches
deep (10 cm). Lightly dust it with flour. Wash and dry the lemons. Grate the zest and chop it finely
(or use a microplane to grate it). Whip the butter with the sugar by hand or with an electric beater
until pale and creamy. Incorporate the vanilla powder or vanilla extract. Sift the flour with the baking
powder. Add one-third of the dry ingredients and 1 egg and combine well. Repeat the procedure
twice, scraping down the sides of the bowl each time to combine all the ingredients. Mix in the lemon
zest. Pour the batter into the cake pan and bake for about 45 minutes, until the top is browned
and a cake tester comes out dry. If the cake browns too much, cover it with parchment paper until
it is done. Turn it out of the pan and let cool on a rack.

For the syrup: Squeeze the 2 lemons and strain the juice. Gently bring the juice, sugar, and water to a boil, until the sugar has just melted. Remove from heat and let cool.

Cut the cool sponge into four rounds of the same thickness. Brush each round with the syrup. Cover a sponge round with one-third of the lemon curd. Carefully place another sponge round on top and repeat the procedure twice, ending with a plain sponge round. Dust generously with confectioners' sugar.

Sometimes, I cover the sponge with white fondant icing and decorate the cake with half a candied cherry, placed in the center. ❧

*I always add vanilla to heighten the flavors.

Christmas Pudding
A MATTER OF TASTE

*More than just a tradition, the inimitable Christmas pudding holds
a special place in British affection. The basic method for making it may not
vary greatly, but no one can claim that there is such a thing as
a single "true" recipe: everyone makes their own adaptations and variations,
so as to reproduce the flavors and memories of their childhood.
Traditionally the pudding would be made a month ahead of Christmas,
on "Stir-up Sunday," when every member of the family would take turns to stir
the mixture while making a wish. James learned about Christmas pudding
from Monsieur Legros. Head chef to the Duke of Windsor, who took him
with him when he left England, Monsieur Legros was a patriarch with an
imposing mustache whose experience working at Buckingham Palace meant
he was an authority on all the great secrets of traditional British cuisine.
No Christmas pudding recipe could be more authentic than that of
Monsieur Legros. Yet none of the ten ambassadors' wives for whom James has
worked has thought it beyond improvement, and some have even given him tips
handed down from their own grandmothers. In the end, James concocted
his own recipe, a combination of them all.
Equally controversial is the question of what should be served with the pudding.
Brandy butter is the most favored accompaniment, but how should it be made?
Sir Christopher Soames liked it made with granulated sugar,
so that it had a slight crunch; Lady Fretwell preferred brown sugar and rum;
and Sir Reginald Hibbert was a champion of icing sugar. Zabaglione
or custard, although more unorthodox, might also be served. One thing everyone
agreed on, however, was that the pudding must arrive at the table in flames.
Traditionally, the hot steamed pudding is decorated with a sprig of holly stuck
in the top, given a liberal dousing with warmed brandy,
set alight, and brought into the dining room to a chorus of
"We wish you a merry Christmas."*

173

CHRISTMAS PUDDING

When I began working at the Embassy, I kept the recipe that we used at the Duke and Duchess of Windsor's residence. After that, each ambassador's wife gave me her grandmother's recipe, and I realized that each family in Britain had its own secret! Finally, I combined several recipes and, judging by the compliments I received from the ambassadors and their guests, I think my recipe is quite a success. This pudding is very easy to make—all you have to do is follow the steps as they are set out here and not over-mix, because otherwise the texture will not be right. You can make it months ahead, even a whole year, as long as you keep it in a cool, dry place.

Serves 6 to 8

INGREDIENTS

1 small carrot, grated (2 oz./50 g)
1 ¾ oz. (40 g) walnuts
1 ½ oz. (35 g) candied orange peel
1 ½ oz. (35 g) candied lemon peel
7 oz. (200 g) currants
7 oz. (200 g) golden raisins (sultanas)
1 ¼ cups (2 ½ oz./75 g) fresh breadcrumbs
6 tablespoons (2 ½ oz./75 g) margarine
   (formerly suet was used)

¾ cup (2 ½ oz./75 g) all-purpose flour, sifted
⅓ cup (2 ½ oz./75 g) light brown sugar
1 drop bitter almond extract
1 heaping teaspoon four spice mixture
   (combine ginger, cinnamon, nutmeg, and cloves)
1 cup (250 ml) beer
1 cup (250 ml) cognac
2 eggs

For the brandy butter

2 sticks (8 oz./250 g) butter, softened
½ cup (3 ½ oz./100 g) sugar or ¾ cup (3 ½ oz./100 g)
   confectioners' sugar*
Scant ½ cup (100 ml) cognac

To flambé

1 tablespoon plus 1 teaspoon (20 ml) cognac

SPECIAL EQUIPMENT
A well-buttered, rounded mold, diameter 6 inches (15 cm) and a deep dish for serving (so that you can safely flambé the cognac when you pour it over the pudding).

Peel and grate the carrot. Chop the walnuts. Dice the orange and lemon peel. In a large mixing bowl, combine the currants, sultanas, breadcrumbs, margarine, flour, sugar, grated carrot, walnuts, candied peel, bitter almond extract, and spices. Cover with a cloth and let rest for about 12 hours in a cool place.

Quickly stir in the beer and cognac, without over-mixing. Cover with a cloth and let macerate for 24 hours in the refrigerator.

Break the eggs and beat them lightly. Stir them into the batter. Butter the pudding mold and fill it to the top with the mixture. Cover with a disk of parchment paper. Above that, place a piece of fabric the size of a table napkin and tie it tightly around the mold with twine. Fold the two opposite corners over the top and tie them in a tight knot. Repeat with the other two corners.

CHRISTMAS PUDDING (continued)

Place the mold in a small pot, add water a quarter way up the mold, and bring to a boil. Simmer gently for 5 hours, adding water from time to time as the simmering water evaporates. Remove from the pot and let the pudding cool. Store in a cool, dry place.

Two hours before serving, reheat the pudding just as you cooked it. Alternatively, you can reheat it in the microwave oven.

Make the brandy butter: Make sure the butter is very soft. Leave it out of the refrigerator in a warm place before you need it.

With a hand whisk or an electric beater, whisk the butter with the sugar until smooth and creamy. Gradually pour in the cognac, whisking until the consistency is very light and foamy.

To serve, turn the hot pudding out onto a round, deep dish. Heat the cognac, pour it over the pudding, and carefully holding a long match, set it alight. Bring the pudding, still flaming, to the table. Serve with the brandy butter.

Some people decorate the pudding with a little branch of holly, but I find it unpleasant to eat a good pudding with an ashy taste. 🍃

* One of the ambassadors asked me to use brown sugar when I prepared the brandy butter so that it was a little crunchy. Instead of brandy butter, you can prepare a crème anglaise with cognac.

PAGES 178-79 *The Ballroom*
of the British Ambassador's Residence in Paris
decorated for Christmas dinner.

SUMMER PUDDING

This is the adaptation of summer pudding I made using raw fruit,
to serve in individual portions at the Embassy.

Prepare a day ahead

Serves 6

INGREDIENTS

1 lb. 2 oz. (500 g) strawberries	4 oz. (125 g) redcurrants
8 oz. (250 g) raspberries	1 genoise sponge, 2 inches (5 cm) thick,
4 oz. (125 g) blueberries	16 x 6 inches (40 x 16 cm), weighing 12 oz. (350 g)
4 oz. (125 g) mulberries	6 slices toasted brioche
	1 bunch redcurrents and mint leaves to serve

For the ice cream

3 cups (750 ml) whole milk	⅔ cups (4 ½ oz./125 g) sugar
¾ vanilla bean, slit lengthwise	1 cup (250 ml) crème fraîche
10 egg yolks	2 tablespoons (30 ml) elder flower syrup

SPECIAL EQUIPMENT

Six dariole molds, diameter 2 ¼ inches (5.5 cm) and depth 2 inches (5 cm) and six disks
of parchment paper, diameter 2 inches (5 cm).

Wash the strawberries carefully, pat them dry, and hull them. Cut them into small pieces.
Cut the raspberries into quarters and the blueberries, mulberries, and redcurrants into halves.

Cut the sponge horizontally into slices about ⅛ inch (4 mm) thick. Cut out six 1 ¾-inch (4 cm)
diameter disks for the bottom of the molds. Then cut six 2-inch (5 cm) disks for the middle and
six 2 ¼-inch (5.5 cm) disks to close the puddings.

Place a disk of parchment paper at the bottom of each mold. Place a 1 ¾-inch (4 cm) disk of
sponge over the lining. Then spoon in a 2-inch (5 cm) layer of berries. Place a 2-inch (5 cm) disk
over the fruit. Spoon in another 2-inch (5 cm) layer of fruit (the molds will be overflowing) and
top with a 2 ¼-inch (5.5 cm) disk. In each mold, in total, there should be three layers of sponge
and two layers of fruit.

Place the molds in a fairly high-sided dish, because the berries will exude a lot of juice. Cover
them with another dish and weigh it down with a weight of about 3 lb. (1.5 kg). Chill for 24 hours.

Make the ice cream: Heat the milk with the vanilla bean. In a mixing bowl, whisk or beat the
sugar with the egg yolks until the mixture is pale, thick, and creamy. Gradually pour over the hot
milk, whisking constantly. Return the mixture to the saucepan, still stirring constantly. Just before
the custard begins to simmer, remove it from heat. Strain through a fine-mesh sieve into
a mixing bowl and let cool, stirring from time to time. When it has cooled, add the crème fraîche
and elder flower syrup. Process the mixture in an ice cream maker or, if you don't have one, place
the mixing bowl in the freezer and stir from time to time until the mixture reaches the consistency
of ice cream.

To serve, turn each pudding onto the side of the plate. On the other side, place a scoop of ice
cream on a slice of toasted brioche. Drizzle with a little of the juice from the berries. Garnish with
a bunch of redcurrant and a mint leaf.

You can make any flavor ice cream you like using the custard base given here. ❧

The Great Tradition at Home

THE HEIGHT OF REFINEMENT—AND THE DISTINGUISHING FEATURE OF THE GREAT TRADITION—IS THE creation of perfection in the guise of apparent simplicity. No longer the exclusive preserve of the elite few who can afford to employ their own chef, this is a form of perfection that can set anyone dreaming.

The world has changed, but this great tradition is now within the reach of many more people than before. Men and women of all backgrounds are now cooking for pleasure and relaxation, and they want to learn from the great chefs. Television cookery series and cookery courses are multiplying and flourishing.

Marie-Blanche de Broglie, who teaches the French *art de vivre* to young women from all over the world, offers the key to this new way of entertaining: "You give what you know how to do, but you give." Simplification and refinement can go together, hand in hand. Elegance may be found in a prettily dressed table in a color palette that simply wasn't possible in the days of damask and lace tablecloths.

Nowadays there is no need to present your guests with a succession of different dishes and courses. If you serve generous aperitif snacks with pre-dinner drinks then you can drop the appetizer altogether, for instance. You can build a menu around a wine, which will automatically give the evening a theme, though this is easier when you have eight guests or more. Distinctive ingredients such as rabbit, pork, and shellfish are best avoided, and caution should be exercised with dishes that are too rich (everyone is watching their weight these days) or contain alcohol (your guests may be driving). The key to a successful dinner lies in the choice of main course. To help in this choice, James shares in this book the secrets of a career spanning fifty-eight years, offering tips to help any aspiring cook follow the recipes he has created for one of the most select and distinguished tables in Paris.

*J*ames Viaene receives the Légion d'honneur

Just once in forty years, James Viaene left his pots and pans behind and emerged from his kitchen. He chose the menu, but on this occasion he sat at the ambassador's table and dined among many distinguished guests, including the French Prime Minister, François Fillon, and all living ambassadors and their spouses. It was November 16, 2010, the day when, thirty-one years after receiving the Médaille d'Or des Cuisiniers Français, he was invested by François Fillon with the insignia of the Légion d'honneur: France's most prestigious distinction for this great chef who was "appreciated and respected by all, and who displayed the highest standards, a deep love for his work, and a profound concern for the human relationships that are formed around the table."

This was not merely a splendid occasion but also a schedule-defying feat, as that day also happened to feature a cabinet reshuffle, and the President of the Republic needed his prime minister! But François Fillon arranged matters so that he could be there nonetheless, in order to honor "the career of an outstanding chef." Recalling that la diplomatie de bouche (dinner-table diplomacy) "used to be viewed as a weapon," he observed that it has now "found its rightful place in an international contest in which each country seeks to defend its place in the world by means of its finest traditions."

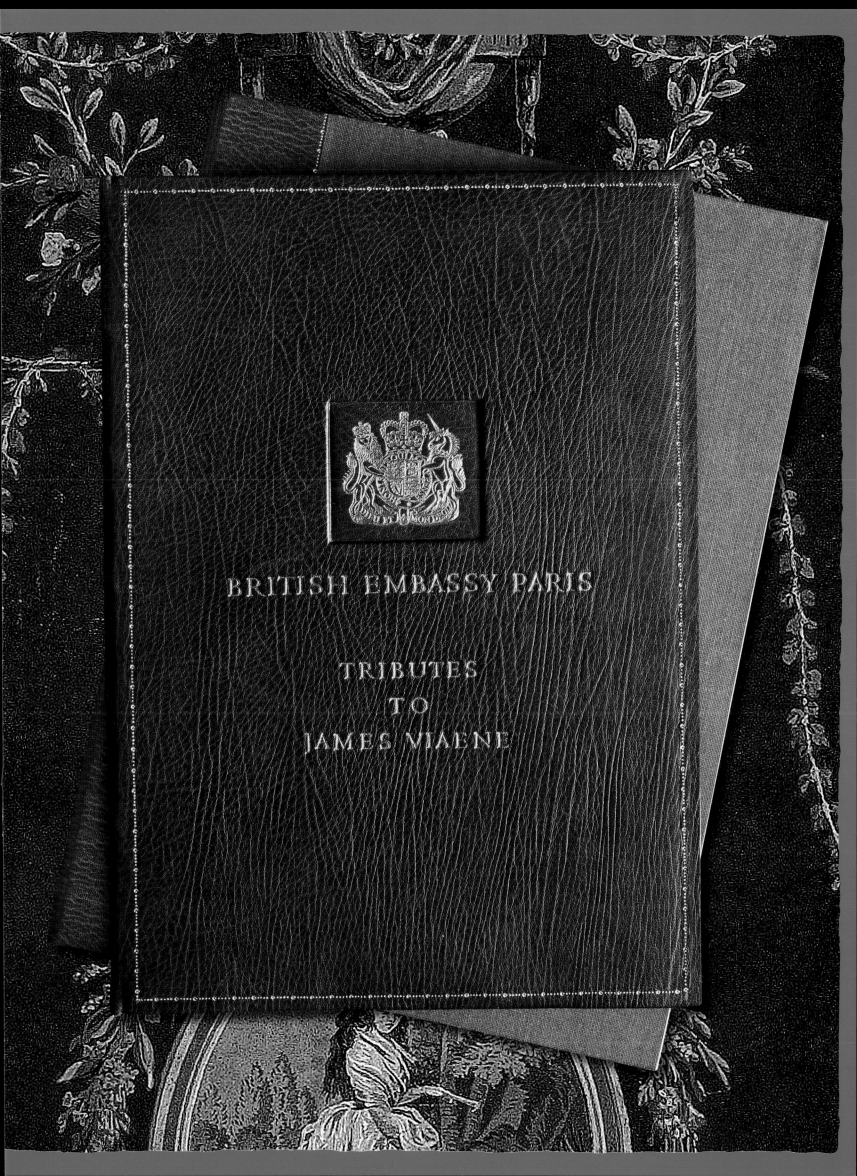

BRITISH EMBASSY PARIS

TRIBUTES
TO
JAMES VIAENE

$\mathcal{I}$ndex of recipes

Acknowledgments

Gratitude fills us with rejoicing, for it so rarely finds frank expression.
STEFAN ZWEIG

It would have been impossible to write this book without Lady Westmacott.
Her enthusiasm and trust were a valuable support throughout the preparation of this book.
I would like to express my warmest gratitude to Sir and Lady Soames who were the first
to entrust me with the kitchens of the British Ambassador's Residence in Paris.
All the ambassadors who succeeded each other during my forty-one years working
at the Embassy renewed this confidence. I send them my warmest gratitude.
For their dedication and professionalism, I would like to thank my kitchen staff.
I am very thankful to l'Académie Culinaire de France for welcoming me in its great family,
particularly Gérard Dupont, President, and my two sponsors, Jean Meunier and Pierre Cecillon.
Thank you to my employers for having shared their invaluable culinary savoir faire with me.
Special thanks to Roger Harmand, pioneer of modern cooking, who helped and
inspired me to invent my own cuisine.
For their time and assistance, special thanks to Suzanne Tise-Isoré, Nadège Forestier,
Francis Hammond, Sarah Rozelle, and Carmela Abramowitz who helped me
immortalize my wonderful culinary adventure in this book.
Finally, I am very thankful to my mother who gave me the desire to cook.

JAMES VIAENE

I express my warmest gratitude to Pierre Barillet, Marie-Blanche de Broglie,
Hélène David-Weill, Monique Raimond, Philippine de Rothschild, and Maryvonne Pinault
who helped me understand the mysteries of Parisian life from 1950 to today.
For their great knowledge of French cooking and beautiful tables: Jean Solanet,
Pierre Emmanuel Taittinger, Jean Meunier, and Ben Newick.
And finally, special thanks to Esmeralda de Tracy and Philomène de Souza Lage
for sharing memories of their father and husband, Jean de Souza Lage.

NADÈGE FORESTIER

.

FACING PAGE *James Viaene asked for his first
and only passport in 1954 in order to go and work
at the French Embassy in London.*

188

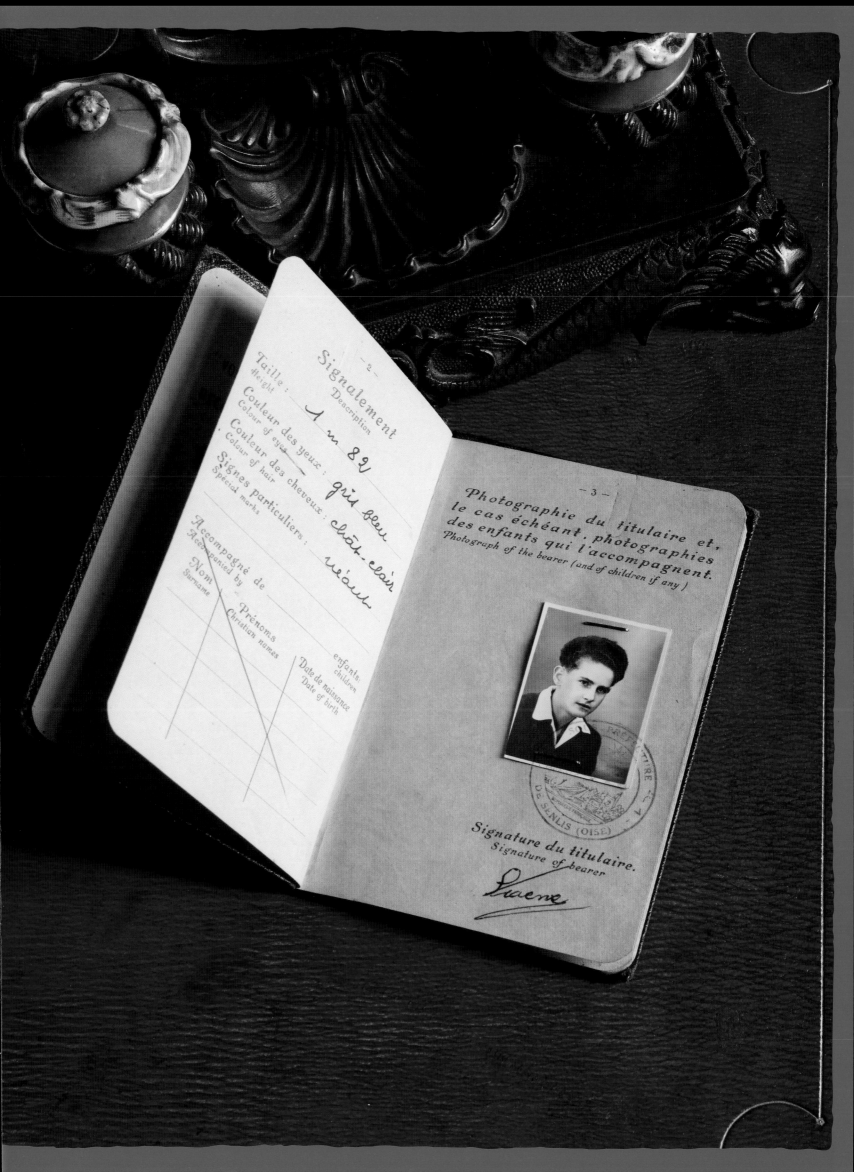

$\mathcal{P}$hotographic Credits

All photographs in this book were taken by Francis Hammond with the exception
of the following: pp. 10, 12, and 13: Robert Doisneau/Rapho; p. 14: © André Ostier;
p. 15: © Georges Saad/L'Art et la Mode, 1952; p. 18: Private collection/All rights reserved;
p. 27: © Maurice Tabard/JWL/She, Camera Press London; p. 29: © Henri Cartier-Bresson/
Magnum Photos; p. 32: Private collection/All rights reserved; p. 33: © William Lovelace/
Express/Getty Images; pp. 34 and 35: © William Vandivert/Time Life Pictures/Getty Images;
p. 47: © The Pepin Press; pp. 51, 52, and 53: Private collection/All rights reserved;
p. 55: © Rue des Archives/AGIP; p. 56: © Rue des Archives/PVDE; p. 57: © Rue des Archives/
AGIP; p. 70: © Jack Nisberg/Roger-Viollet; p. 85: © Depositphotos/Patrick Guénette;
p. 91: © Depositphotos/Patrick Guénette; p. 99: © The Pepin Press; p. 116: © The Pepin
Press; p. 117: © Picture Post/Hulton Archive/Getty Images; p. 119: © The Pepin Press;
p. 132: © Depositphotos/Patrick Guénette; p. 133 (photograph): © Studio Lipnitzki/Roger-
Viollet; p. 144: © Depositphotos/Ela Kwasniewski; p. 145: BNF; p. 155: Courtesy of the
Cecil Beaton Studio Archive at Sotheby's; p. 159: iStockphoto; p. 161: Clipart Courtesy FCIT;
p. 162: © Depositphotos/Patrick Guénette; p. 177: © Depositphotos/Patrick Guénette.
The folio decorations are from iStockphoto.

PAGE 192 *The residence of the British*
Ambassador in Paris at dusk.